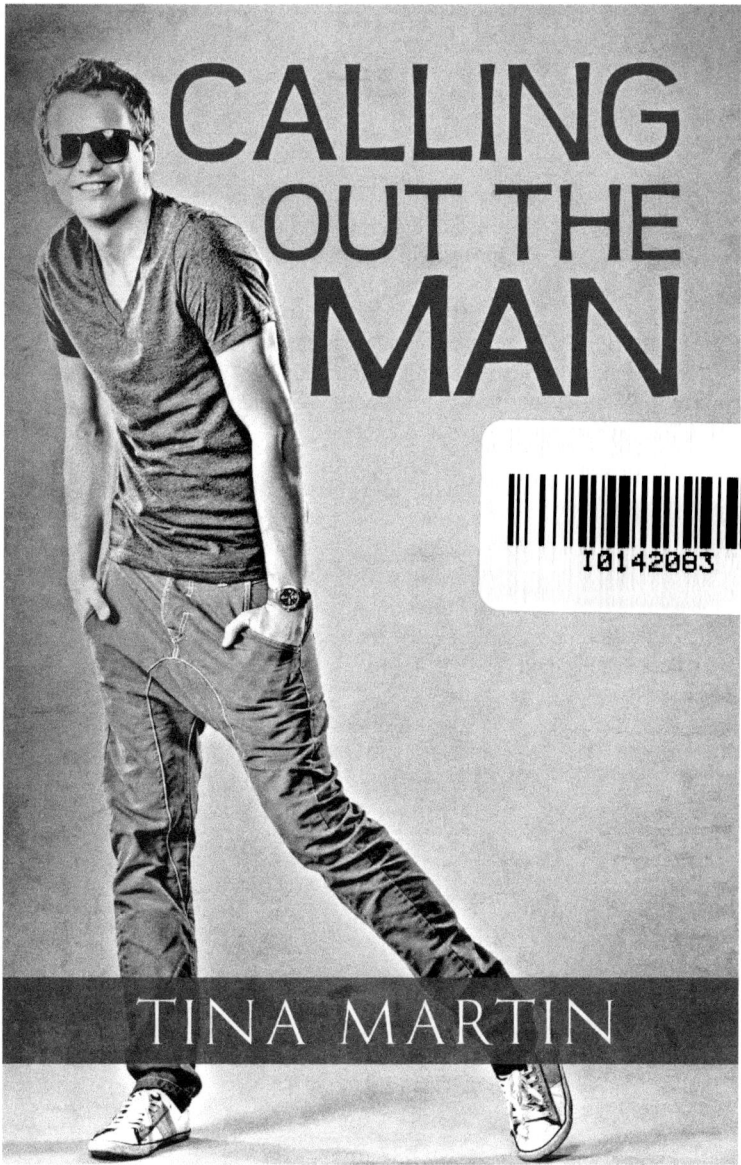

CALLING OUT THE MAN

TINA MARTIN

CALLING OUT THE MAN

21st Century Press is a Christian publisher dedicated to publishing books
with high family values. We believe the vision for 21st Century Press is
to provide families and individuals with user-friendly materials that will
help them in their daily lives and experiences.

It is our hope that this book will help you discover truths for your own
life and help you meet the needs of others. May you be richly blessed

21st Century Press
2131 W. Republic Rd. PMB 211
Springfield, MO 65807
800-658-0284
www.21stcenturypress.com

ISBN: 978-0-9911004-7-7
Cover Design: Lee Fredrickson
Book Design: Lee Fredrickson
Photo of Tina Martin: Michelle Oshel Woods of Backwoods
Photography (Bolivar, MO 417 298 2994)

21stCENTURY
P   R   E   S   S
READING YOU LOUD AND CLEAR.

DEDICATION

I would like to first of all dedicate this book to my God whose unfailing love, even when I am not very loveable, never ceases. You are my rock and my salvation forever and always.

Second, I would like to dedicate this book to the beat of my heart, my son, Samuel Dale Martin.

You were named after the Prophet and last of the Judges in the Bible, Samuel. Samuel was a man chosen for God from his amazing and miraculous birth until his dying breath. Samuel served in a multitude of important positions throughout his life and because he knew how to obey he earned God's favor. He served the Lord with integrity and faith that was unwavering and strong. Few people in all of the Old Testament were as loyal to God as Samuel. Samuel showed that obedience and respect are the best ways in which to show our God we love Him.

Samuel was a man of honor.

Son, that's a big role model to live up to! You're already on the right path though and I am so blessed to be your mother. Before you were born I prayed and told God I would dedicate you to Him. It's my prayer that the words of this book will guide you into becoming a REAL man of Godly character and integrity.

Though many call me mom, only you can truly call me momma.

I love you so much!

Michael

CONTENTS

Introduction

CALLING OUT THE MAN

I saw a movie once in which a group of men were sitting around talking about life. One man asked the rest if they remembered when they knew they had become a man. As each of them answered, one particular answer got me thinking. The man simply said, "When my father called the man out in me." The movie is called Courageous and it's one I would highly recommend any man of any age to watch.

Over the last several years God has placed several boys in my life through my youth ministry who have come from homes where the father figure has had little or no involvement. What little involvement there was usually had a very negative effect on the boy. I believe much of what boys learn about becoming a man has to do with what their fathers teach them. So what about these boys whose fathers are not there to advise or teach them how to be a man? Who calls out the man in them?

That's what this book is about. With input from coaches, teachers, and many Godly men and women I am offering advice on how to be a man of great character. So to answer my own question, "Who calls out the man in a boy whose earthly father wasn't there to call him out? Answer: his Heavenly Father through the wisdom of those who love Him.

"Choose my instruction rather than silver, and knowledge rather than pure gold. For wisdom is far more valuable than rubies. Nothing you desire can compare with it" (Proverbs 8:10-11).

(Coach Clayton McCullah) "What does it mean to be a man? To be considered 'manly' or 'tough?' That's a good question. The world's view of a man, in my opinion, sends a poor message to boys and adolescent males trying to determine what a man really is."

The Hamar tribe in Ethiopia place great value on cattle. The boys in the tribe take part in a ceremony in order to become a man. They line the cattle up for bull jumping. This is the last test they must pass before becoming a man and getting married. Basically what takes place is the tribe forms a circle around the cows. The women are whipped to prove courage and in order to accompany a young man during the ceremony. The young man comes naked to the ceremony, jumps on a bull, then starts running across the back of the cattle. If he makes it without falling off he is then considered a man. If he falls, he is whipped, ridiculed and shamed the rest of his life.

The Bullet Ant of the Amazon Rainforest is known as one of the nastiest types of ants. Its name refers to the fact that a sting from one of these ants feels like getting shot with a bullet. Bullet ant's stings are the worst in the insect world. The Satere MawÄ people sew these ants into wicker gloves with the stingers pointing inward. Their young men, some as young as twelve, then put on these gloves containing hundreds if not thousands of Bullet Ants. The boys then must dance around wearing the gloves for anywhere from ten minutes to a half hour. They don't just do this one time though but twenty!

You don't need a ceremony to tell you when you are a man. Sometimes you just need to know what a real man is.

When asked if they knew when you became a man, a group of boys replied with the following answers:

- When you get your first job.

- When you start getting body hair.

- When you have sex.

- When you get married.

- When you start driving.

- When you turn eighteen.

- When you go to college.

- When you develop big muscles.

The world wants to give us a trashy version of what a real man is. I want to give you a true vision of a real man.

- A real man does the right thing even when no one is watching and no praise will come his way. They follow rules.

- A real man will be honest and will keep his promises.

- A real man will work hard and take care of what he has and anything that is entrusted to him.

- A real man is loyal. He stands by the people he loves.

He knows who is important in his life and he cherishes them.

- A real man will respect and honor the girls and women in his life. He will not degrade them or let anyone else.

- A real man protects his mind. He doesn't let trash infiltrate it. He's careful about the media he fills his mind with.

- A real man honors marriage and waits to give his heart and body to his wife. He understands this is a precious gift that should only be given to her. He commits to God, his wife, family and friends to stay married to one woman for life.

- A real man loves God with all his heart, mind, strength, and soul. He spends time reading his Bible and talking to God. He attends church regularly and grows in his relationship with God above all else.

- A real man is not afraid of his feelings and knows his own heart well. He's not afraid of sharing his feelings with others.

- A real man is courageous and strong. He protects others and will sacrifice himself for them.

(Coach Lance W. Roweton) "Never stop improving yourself. I look at myself as a work in progress. I believe everyone in this world has qualities I want to possess and qualities that I don't. I study literally every person I am around and try to gain from them the qualities that I wish to possess. I got my calm demeanor from my Grandpa Roweton. I got my business ambition from my Dad. I got my tough-minded quality from my dad. My competitiveness is from Dad and my brothers. My quiet confidence is from my Dad. The way I talk to kids on a regular basis when I am coaching is a quality I learned from Ronnie Evans, a coach I coached with at Willard High School. Kids loved to play for him and I wanted kids to love to play for me.

Part of the way I conduct my football program is from Chris Church, the band director at Willard. He still has one of the best programs around. I used to get to school early and sit in my classroom and listen to the way he conducted his band practices because I wanted to be successful like him.

My list goes on and on of people who have influenced me one way or another. How long is your list? I have found that successful people learn from other successful people...and once you have made a success of yourself remember it is the important people that don't mind acting unimportant.... We all need a foundation from which to draw from when it comes to making it in the game of life... I am going to share some thoughts about various topics that have helped me with my own personal journey. I am not an old man so my journey is far from over. I have not made it but feel I am making it because of the men I have modeled myself after. The men who helped me become a man. I am not your father, but I hope when you reflect back on your transition into manhood, you will think of me as one of the men that helped you get there."

"When I was a child, I spoke and thought and reasoned as a child. But when I grew up, I put away childish things" (1 Corinthians 13:11).

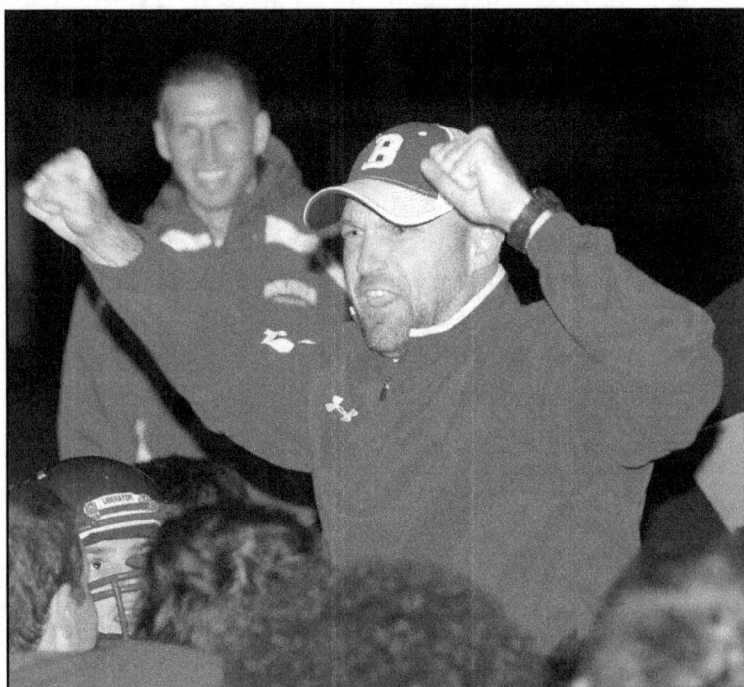

Coach Lance Roweton

Chapter 1

INTEGRITY

"The righteous who walks in his integrity-
blessed are his children after him! Even a child
makes himself known by his acts, by whether his
conduct is pure and upright" (Proverbs 20:7, 11).

Over the last several years I have encountered teenage
boys who have come from horrific home lives. Instead of a nurturing and loving environment, many of them
experienced things no child should ever have to endure.
Abuse and neglect have been their prime lessons in life.
The lessons of manipulation, lying, anger and control are
planted in their hearts and minds. It amazes me to see how
God has blessed me with the right gardening tools to root
out these weeds and replace them with seeds of hope.

The young men brought into my life will often hear me
say the first thing they need to do is give their life to God,
believe in Him and repent. The Bible tells us in 2 Corinthians 5:17, "This means that anyone who belongs to Christ
has become a new person. The old life is gone; a new life
has begun!"

So many kids come to me broken and beaten down by the things they have already done in their lives in which they are completely ashamed of. They feel hopeless and have a hard time forgiving themselves. God is ready to begin a new creation. He is just waiting for them to take that step of faith and be willing to put their old lives behind them and move forward into creating a new one.

(Papa & Granny) "Hold your head high and be proud of who you are. Never put a bad mark on your name."

Papa Glenn Walton

One of the biggest areas I really encourage kids to grow in is integrity. To me this defines who your character really is. I remember as a kid going back to the little town in Arkansas where my daddy and his family grew up. My dad could go anywhere in that town and start visiting with someone. Sooner or later someone would ask his name and then our family's character would be revealed.

"Oh, you're Virgil Walton's boy? He was a good honest man."

You see back when my father was growing up a man's word and a hand shake were all you needed. If you kept your word and lived a life of integrity, your family name was as good as gold. They knew you did what you said you were going to do and you did it to the best of your ability.

Because of my grandfather's integrity, to this day my children can go back to that little town and their family name will be recognized as something of value.

This is something anyone can create. It's a matter of choice and it's not always easy. But it can start with you and will trickle down through your children and many generations to come.

> (Coach Bayless) "Integrity is what you do when no one else is watching. A truly honest man has this because he is driven from the inside by his integrity. A man with integrity earns a good name because he does things, big and small, without expecting a reward, but because what he does is simply the right thing to do."

Pretty basic: Integrity is just doing the right thing. People can turn a blind eye to what is right or pretend they don't know. Maybe they would rather try to take the easy way out. I believe deep down our basic instincts tell us what the right thing to do is. If you are truly having problems knowing what is right, then ask those people in your life you trust the most.

Don't always expect praise and attention for doing what is right. Just do it because you know it is right. Believe me; people sometimes will notice that more than the person who is always waving around awards.

> (Rick Warren) "Integrity is built by defeating the temptation to be dishonest; humility grows when we refuse to be prideful; and endurance develops every time you reject the temptation to give up."

Reuben Gonzales grew up on the streets as part of a gang. Life was not easy for him but one thing he enjoyed and became very good at was playing wall ball. As time went on he realized this gift he had was his ticket out of the rough life he grew up with. Gonzales joined the pro racquetball tour in 1981 and was known to have a ferocious determination. It was in 1985 though, that the world got to see what kind of man he really was. He was in the final match of a professional tournament in which it would be his first opportunity at a victory on the pro circuit, and he was playing against the perennial champion. In the fourth and final game, right at match point, Gonzales made a super "kill" shot into the front wall to win it all! The referee called it good. The crowd went wild! One of the two linesmen affirmed that the shot was in. But....Gonzales, after a moment's hesitation, turned around, shook his opponent's hand, and declared that his shot had hit the floor first. As a result, he lost the match. He walked off the court. Everybody was stunned. Who could ever imagine it in any sport or endeavor? A player with everything officially in his favor, with victory in his hand, disqualified himself at match point and lost!

When asked why he did it, Reuben said, "It was the only thing I could do to maintain my INTEGRITY." Gonzales realized that he could always win another match, but he could never regain his lost integrity. According to pro Jerry Hilecher, "What he did gave Reuben lasting respect from the other players and the fans. His message was that winning's not as important as integrity and having pride in yourself."

(Griff) "Treat everyone you meet with respect, even if they haven't earned it and especially when they don't deserve it. Just because they treat you badly, does not give you the right to return the favor. 'Kill 'em with kindness.'"

Griff Schoen

How you treat others will reveal your character and integrity. We often hear the saying, "treat others how you would want to be treated." Over the years that saying has almost become a thing of the past. I think the message now a days is, "treat others how they have treated you." We live in a "get even" society. I don't believe we should be a doormat for anyone. I do think we should learn to look at others through the eyes of God. What makes us so perfect? We mess up time and time again, and are forgiven, yet we expect perfection out of others. It's so easy whenever someone has hurt you to want to run them down or hurt them back. Basically, all you are doing then is acting just like them. Raise your standards and take the high road. It won't make you feel any better about yourself to get even. In all honesty you will more than likely feel worse. Anger and resentment sets in and slowly starts destroying your heart. When you can look at someone who has hurt you and still show respect, then you are the one setting a high standard for them to look up to. They are unable to hold anything against you.

(Ken Freed) "Integrity, Honesty and Faithfulness are the three most important things… You must guard these three like it is the gold in Ft. Knox."

We look at our lives and often place value on things or people. If we were to guard our integrity as much as we guard our most prized possession, think of how strong our character would be! The world wants to steal, kill and destroy things like integrity, honesty and faithfulness. It wants us to believe it has better things to offer. It laughs and says, "YOLO! Do whatever YOU want to do. Don't worry about what others think or feel!" But instead, what we end up with are feelings of shame, disappointment, emptiness, sickness, and hurt.

(Gina Green) "Every decision that you make will have an effect on your life. Everything in your life that is worth complaining about or being happy about is a direct result of a choice that you made. So, make good choices. Take the advice of the people who love you when you need help."

Your life is about choices. You choose whether or not you want to be a man of integrity or just another guy who never grew up. You know the type I'm talking about. The one who instead of taking care of his children and family decides to blow all his money in a new tattoo business of his own and tries it out on friends or has to have the latest "toy" to play with instead of providing food, shelter, clothing and, most of all, love to his own family.

Sometimes it can be very hard to know how to make the right choices. There are things you can do to help you. One of the biggest things you can do before making a choice is to just stop what you're doing and pray. If you earnestly pray about it, God will give you the guidance you need. Really, think about what you are doing before you do it. Think about the results and what they could be. Don't do anything rash. You have to decide if the choice you're about to make will affect others in a good or bad way, and how in turn that will affect you. When I say don't do anything rash I mean don't do something out of feelings of the moment. Take some time to really think it through. Spend a few days thinking about it. Ask others their opinion. Most of all don't do anything when you are in a very emotional state.

> (Coach Clayton McCullah) "Real men have strength of character. True strength, the ability to withstand trials and tribulations comes from strength of character and an understanding that life is going to knock you down, but you are defined by your resiliency and determination to keep getting up. One of my favorite quotes is from Michael Josephson. He said, '**People of character do the right thing even if no one else is, not because they think it will change the world, but because they refuse to be changed by the world.**' Real men have integrity. This goes right along with strength of character. They do what's right because it's right. Remember...what's popular isn't always right and what's right isn't always popular. Men know this, but it doesn't deter them from doing the right thing...even if it is hard or unpopular to do."

Most of your choices will have a ripple effect for the rest of your life. Sometimes it may feel as if it would be easier to blame others for what happens in your life, but the truth is you control the direction you're going. You do this by all the small choices you make every day. You choose when you get up and when you go to sleep. You choose what you put on and in your body. You choose what you fill your mind with and the people you want to interact with. You choose to be kind and to be happy. The choices you make will have an impact on the quality of life you live and the type of character you will obtain. The strongest men have often times had to make the most unpopular choices, but choices they knew where the right thing to do.

(Kwasi Ofori-Yeboah) "The saying goes that there are only two certainties in life; death and taxes, everything else can be unpredictable, including people. However, there are people with integrity who will stand by their word and the world would definitely be a better place if we had more people with integrity. Integrity has been defined as adhering to moral and ethical principles. It has also been defined as doing the right thing when no one is watching. I will encourage you to strive to be a man of integrity for it will serve you well in life. Even in the face of adversity and hardships and when everyone else is doing the contrary, sticking to your principles will always lead to vindication. Friends and foes alike will come to admire your strength of character as a man of integrity. Integrity, don't live life without it."

Other people can try and hold your hand through life and continue to tell you what is right, and what is wrong. When you practice integrity it becomes natural to you. It becomes a part of who you are. Knowing what's right and what's wrong will be implanted in your heart. Choosing to do what's right is not always easy. Sometimes you have to look at what is at risk.

Real Men Have Integrity.

Chapter 2

HONESTY

"Judge nothing before the appointed time: wait until the Lord comes. He will bring to light what is hidden in darkness and will expose the motives of the heart. At that time each will receive their praise from God" (1 Corinthians 4:5).

(Coach Daniel Bayless) "There is no such thing as a little lie. I once heard a story about a guy playing cards. He lied about what was in his hand. A lady called him out on it and asked him if he knew he had destroyed the value of his name with his lie. The man said, 'It is just a little lie, it doesn't mean anything.' She replied, 'How tragic, your name means so little that you would tarnish it over something that does not mean anything.'"

L ying. This one personally gets to me. Everyone wants to be trusted and for some reason we all think we deserve other peoples trust without really earning it. Then we lie and don't understand why the person we lied to no longer trusts us. The sad part is, most of the time, what we lied about could have been completely avoided or the simple truth told. Lying is a coward's way of dealing with life. It takes real courage to tell the truth. One of the biggest excuses for lying I have heard told over and over is, "Well, I didn't want to hurt you." Let's think about this. Finding out someone broke your trust will hurt them far more than what was being lied about. More than likely if you are lying about something, it is because you are doing something you know is not right. Just don't do it, plain and simple! What? Is that groans and eye rolling taking place? Yeah, I know. Sometimes it's not so simple. But here's where you need to grow up and think about others more than yourselves. I say this in all love and not meanly. Everyone, at some point in their life, has been dishonest. The key is to learn from that mistake and to open your eyes to the problems it caused and do your best not to repeat it.

Insanity: doing the same thing over and over again and expecting different results

(Griff)   "Your word is your bond. Never make a promise if you don't intend to follow through. You don't want to be known as the liar. People you interact with want to know that you are reliable."

If you say you're going to do something, do it. If you say you're going to be somewhere, be there. If you say you're going to help with something, help. If you say you're going to take care of something, take care of it. If you say you're not going to do something, don't do it.

(Barry Farr) "Honesty and integrity are also in short supply these days...the trick is to be honest with yourself: not too hard on yourself, but honest. Face it when you make a mistake, and make it right."

There is an old story about honesty that goes something like this:

There was a king who had gotten very old. The time had come for him to choose who would take his place. Instead of following the custom of choosing his children or his closest aide he called every young man in the country and gave a speech in front of them. "I shall hold a contest. Every one of you will receive a seed. I want you to plant the seed, tend to it, and come back in a year. Whoever has the best plant will be the one I choose as the next king.

A young man named Ethan was very excited about this opportunity. He took his seed, planted it, and watered it every single day. After a month had gone by he noticed that his seed did not seem to be growing. After six months gone by several of the young men were boasting about their plants and how tall and beautiful they were growing, but Ethan's pot was still empty. Ethan didn't say a word to his friends but kept tending to his pot, which was still empty.

The year had passed and all the young men started bringing their tall, beautiful plants before the king. Ethan was embarrassed and ashamed because his pot was still empty. He was reluctant to go before the king, but his mother encouraged him to go and be honest.

The king looked at all the plants brought before him and admired them and praised them saying,

"Your work is outstanding. Your plants are very beautiful indeed. I shall choose one of you to be the new king!"

All of a sudden the king saw Ethan standing at the back of the crowd and shouted to him to come forward with his pot. Ethan was frightened thinking he will surely be killed.

The crowd teased him and insulted him as he carried his empty pot toward the king. "Silence!" The king shouted. The king turned toward Ethan and bowing to him then announced, "Behold your new king!" The crowd was shocked! How could this be? How could someone who completely failed be their new king? The king then continued, "One year ago I gave each one of you a seed to be planted and taken care of. The seed I gave everyone was cooked and could not possibly grow. Every one of you replaced your seed with another. Only Ethan had the honesty and courage to bring the pot with the actual seed I gave him in it. Therefore, he will be your next king."

(Kwasi Ofori-Yeboah) "Honesty they say is the best policy. When asked if she always told the truth, a woman replied, 'Yes, because the truth is always easy to remember.' You are going to come across many situations in life where it will be easier to get away with a fib only to realize that the truth would have served you better in the long run. Make it your goal therefore to stay true to yourself and to let truth guide your conduct and relations with others."

"Oh what a tangled web we weave when first we practice to deceive." Sir Walter Scott

A spider's purpose in spinning a web is to catch prey. Its web is a trap. Whenever something gets caught in its web it is disabled. The spider eventually swoops in and binds the victim and devours it. Webs can look beautiful and delicate; very intricate. Watching a spider spin its web often times is fascinating. But have you ever accidentally walked through a spider's web? Most people want to brush it off of themselves as quickly as possible.

When you intentionally deceive (lying, cheating, etc.), you entangle yourself in a very complicated mess of a situation.

Lying becomes a habit, and a bad habit at that. You start off with a small lie, and then you must tell another lie to cover up that one, and before you know it you have spun a horrible web of deceit. It may look pretty for a little while, but as soon as someone walks through those lies and see's what you have created, they want to brush it off of them immediately.

> "Always tell the Truth. That way, you don't have to remember what you said." ~Mark Twain

> (Coach Clayton McCullah) "Real men stay true to their commitments. Their word is their bond. A handshake is as good as a written contract signed in blood. That goes for everything..."

A man of integrity can look you in the eye and say, "trust me" and you know you can trust him. If you promise someone you will or will not do something and you look them in the eye and ask them to trust you then you better guard that trust like your life is depending on it. It's better to tell the person that you are struggling with whatever it was you promised and see if they can help you than to flat out break their trust. If someone has given their trust to you, they have given you a rare and precious gift of honor. They are saying to you, "I believe in you and I trust you to be loyal to yourself first off, and then to me, the person trusting you."

(Gina Green) "Your reputation depends on your honesty. Lying never gets you where you want to be. It always catches up to you."

Honesty is a reflection of your innermost character, and your character plays a huge role in the direction your life will take.

"...Fix your thoughts on what is true, and honorable, and right, and pure, and lovely, and admirable. Think about things that are excellent and worthy of praise. Keep putting into practice all you learned and received from me-everything you heard from me and saw me doing. The God of peace will be with you" (Philippians 4:8, 9).

Real Men are honest.

Sam's crew

Chapter 3

LOYALTY

"Never let go of loyalty and faithfulness. Tie them around your neck; write them on your heart. If you do this, both God and people will be pleased with you. Trust in the Lord with all your heart. Never rely on what you think you know. Remember the Lord in everything you do, and he will show you the right way. Never let yourself think that you are wiser than you are; simply obey the Lord and refuse to do wrong. If you do, it will be like good medicine, healing your wounds and easing your pains" (Proverbs 3:3-8 GNTA).

(Kwasi Ofori-Yeboah) "Fair weather friends are a dime a dozen, but loyal friends are hard to come by. Choose your friends wisely and when you do, make sure that they can count on your integrity and honesty to be there for all times. Some of these friends will disappoint you just as you might disappoint them, but a loyal friend can be counted on to stand by a friend and you want to be such a friend."

"Do not be misled, 'Bad company corrupts good character" (1 Corinthians 15:33).

Michael's Story

I first knew Michael was a guy of good character while watching him play football, one day, in my front yard with a group of youth. I barely knew this tall, stocky built young man whenever I went up to him that day in the middle of the game and asked him to pretend to fall to the ground when I pretended to deck him one. Without hesitation Michael put on a good show of taking a hit. Everyone was greatly impressed with my strength and power, at least that's what I like to believe, and Michael became a loyal friend.

Loyalty means a lot to Michael and you will understand why when you read his story:

When I was seven years old my parents divorced. It was tough. I thought everything was my fault and I didn't really know what was going on. A couple years later my dad moved back, but not for long. He was gone a lot. I thought he was at work. Come to find out he was having an affair. Over the next couple years there seemed to always be a Uhaul truck in front of our house in case dad wanted to leave. When I was around the age of nine I can remember my parents having a huge fight and then dad was gone for good.

It was really hard on me and my mom. Mom cried a lot and had to work more. She went into a big depression. I had a lot of bad feeling toward my dad. He tore our family apart and it never was the same again. Holidays were really hard on us.

I guess a positive side to all this was I probably wouldn't have been as active in sports or tried as hard in school if I wouldn't have went through all this with my dad leaving. I vowed to myself I would never do anything like that. I told myself I would put everything I had into everything I did. I had to grow up and take on more responsibilities. It also helped me to emotionally mature. I learned how to deal with things differently.

It has been hard though. When I play sports and I see other guys with their dads, that really hurts. Or even going to friends' houses and seeing them with their dads.

The last few years I've been kind of depressed. I feel my dad has missed time with me that he now can never get back. The pain I carry with me from my childhood is just a reminder to stay loyal.

I have trust issues. Because of this I've never really had a girlfriend per se. It is something I desire but I struggle with getting past the trust issues and opening up my heart. I feel like if my dad would have been around and shown loyalty it would have been easier. I probably would have had more confidence. My dad grew up in a broken home and had the same issues. I'm afraid this cycle might continue so I have struggles opening up and trusting others.

A person who has been the biggest influence in my life is my friend Bryce's dad, Rhett Warden. He is, in my opinion, the definition of a family man. He goes to work, comes home. I feel like its mostly the daily witness. He comes home and spends time with his family. I think that's one of the most important things a man can do.

I feel like honesty, loyalty, and integrity are the strongest character traits. Loyalty, can go with friends and teammates and a wife. Being faithful or dedicating yourself to a person or team.

I feel you become a man when you actually understand these things and know who you are and what you are going to do.

I've slipped up here and there. I think that's normal. But I try to stay strong with everything. Sometimes dealing with the past issues brings sadness and depression. I try to look on the bright side and know I have my own future and will do better than what my own dad did.

Anyone who knows me very well will hear these three pieces of advice often.

1. **Know who the important people are in your life.** These are the forever people who will be there for you no matter what. Make them a priority always. Cherish them like none other, and make sure they know you cherish them; not just in words but in how you treat them and the time you make for them. They should *never* doubt how important they are in your life. Don't give permanent feelings to temporary people. Guard your heart for those you cherish.

2. **Friends bring you up and will not pull you down.** If someone is constantly causing you to waver in your morals, getting you into trouble, or making you feel bad about yourself, and not building you up, then that someone is not a real friend.

3. **In the same way make sure you are being the type of friend who brings out the best in someone you care about.** The old saying is so true, "If you want a good friend you must be a good friend." Who you're spending the majority of your time with will reflect on your character. Even if you don't do the negative things they

might be doing, you become associated with them. It's okay to try to help someone who is struggling with life. We are supposed to love everyone and not judge. Jesus talked to some of the lowest people in life. But his close intimate friends were followers of Him. Make sure your loyalty lies with people of good character and integrity.

(Coach Daniel Bayless) "Most people understand a loyal man does not waver in his loyalty. Today, Less people understand the importance of choosing who your loyalty is for. Stand with someone who is right and you will be strong. Weak men stand with the strong, and don't consider who is right."

Sometimes, choosing the person you are going to be loyal to can be very confusing. People change throughout life. Don't choose your loyalty to someone just because you have known them a long time. Take a close look at their character. Are they a Christian? Do they have high standards? Do they encourage you to be your best?

It's easy to find people who will praise you, but sometimes it's the ones who are honest with you when you're heading down a path, you shouldn't be going, that are the more loyal friends. If someone is always agreeing with you no matter the circumstances then more than likely they are not being honest with you. It takes a strong man to do what's right especially when his "friends" are doing what is wrong but having fun doing it. Choose very carefully where your loyalty goes.

(Barry Farr) "Loyalty is also a very rare characteristic in our culture. You can see it in sports, church, business and most aspects of life. People will change for very shallow reasons because loyalty is in short supply. I also want to challenge you to be faithful...Remember that reacting to others failure is not enough; make it your goal to be faithful and loyal to those you love and never choose your own comfort or success over theirs."

"A friend loves at all times, and a brother is born for adversity" (Proverbs 17:17).

A genuine friend loves through the best and worst of times. In fact, a friend's true colors are revealed when we go through unusually difficult or painful circumstances. According to Proverbs it's preferable to have one or two close, intimate companions than a bunch of superficial acquaintances. The person who maintains only surface relationships with a wide number of people may eventually face ruin for lack of good advice when it is really needed. Proverbs 18:24 says, "There are 'friends' who destroy each other, but a real friend sticks closer than a brother." True friends also wound us. They're willing to tell us the hard truth, even when it hurts. We can trust their honest feedback, but an enemy only multiplies kisses. (Proverbs 27:6 "Wounds from a friend can be trusted, but an enemy multiplies kisses.") Beware of someone who doesn't have the courage to confront you when you need it.

"Greater love has no man than this that a man
lay down his life for his friends" (John 15:13).

Laying down your life for others means putting them first and making their needs more important than your own. It means being selfless and sacrificial in your actions towards others rather than selfish.

Again, the people in your life who you truly cherish should see the great love you have for them by the sacrificial actions you show them. This is why it is so important to know where your loyalty stands.

I can't begin to tell you the countless times I have given up my comfort, time, money, and set aside my life for someone else. No, it wasn't easy at all. There were times when I felt alone and misunderstood; times where I felt taken advantage of and used. The amazing thing was that during those times when I was sacrificing for someone else, I found out whom my true friends where: my loyal friends. They were the ones who prayed for me and encouraged me. The ones who listened and gave me a shoulder to cry on when needed. Those friends celebrated in my victories and hurt for me when I hurt. They also were the ones who stood up to me and told me what I needed to hear even when I didn't want to hear it. They never judged me. They just loved me unconditional. When I was worn and weary they didn't burden me more, but offered me comfort. These friends have my trust and loyalty.

Real Men are loyal.

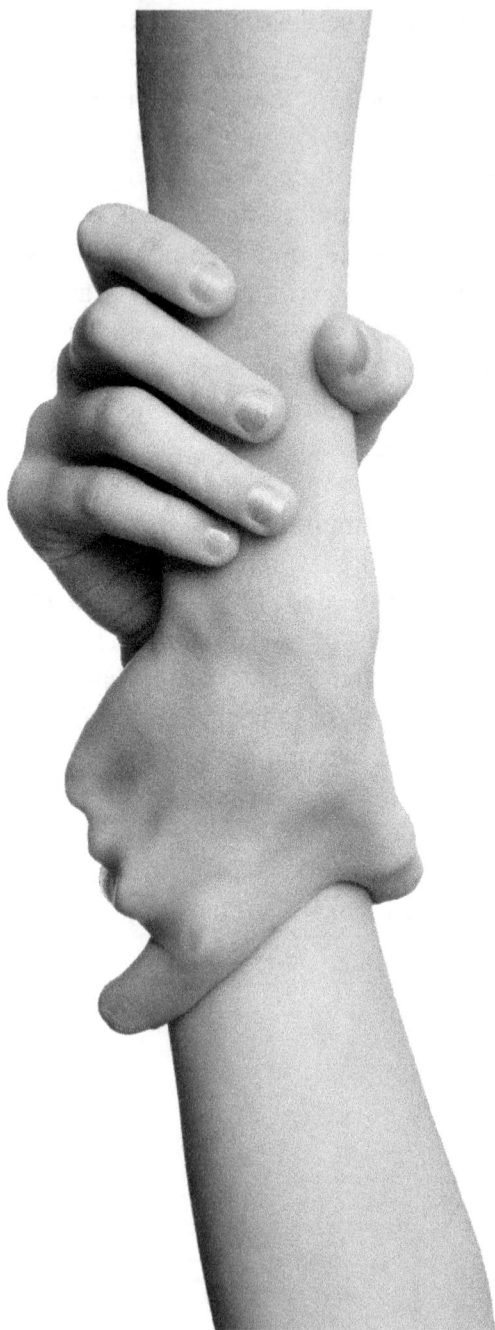

Chapter 4

HUMBLENESS

"So here's what I want you to do, God help-ing you: Take your everyday, ordinary life- your sleeping, eating, going-to-work, and walking-around life-and place it before God as an offering. Embracing what God does for you is the best thing you can do for Him. Don't become so well-adjust-ed to your culture that you fit into it without even thinking. Instead, fix your attention on God. You'll be changed from the inside out. Readily recognize what He wants from you, and quickly respond to it. Unlike the culture around you, always dragging you down to its level of immaturity, God brings the best out of you, develops well-formed maturity in you. I'm speaking to you out of deep gratitude for all that God has given me, and especially as I have responsibilities in relation to you. Living then, as every one of you does, in pure grace, it's important that you not misinterpret yourselves as people who are bringing this goodness to God. No, God brings it all to you. The only accurate way to understand ourselves is by what God is and by what He does for us, not by what we are and what we do for Him" (Romans 12:1-3 MSG).

(Coach Daniel Bayless) "This word is misunderstood all the time. When Jesus said, be humble; He said it in the ancient Greek, and that definition for humbleness is, "power under control." An army following their general's orders into battle is humble. Great athletes are humble (The GREAT ones, the ones who are under control). A powerful battleship with no rudder is a waste, but a ship under control can win a battle, save an army, protect a country. Being humble is controlling your power."

To be humble basically means understanding that the delights, pains, and needs of others are as important as your own, even though they don't feel so. When you are humble, you can laugh at your self-importance and sometimes, even, set it aside. You can see your own faults and the strengths of others, and you recognize how much you have been given, unearned.

(Kwasi Ofori-Yeboah) "Humility has been defined as strength under control. Not thinking more highly of yourself than you ought to, but instead treating every one with respect as you would like to be treated. Giving everyone you meet the benefit of the doubt that they mean well until they prove otherwise. Be firm in your convictions but express them in love and gentleness."

A young lady was waiting for her flight in the boarding room of a big airport. As she would need to wait many hours, she decided to buy a book to spend her time. She also bought a packet of cookies. She sat down in an armchair, in the VIP room of the airport, to rest and read in peace. Beside the armchair where the packet of cookies lay, a man sat down in the next seat, opened his magazine and started reading. When she took out the first cookie, the man took one also. She felt irritated but said nothing. She just thought "What nerve! If I was in the mood I would punch him for being so rude!" For each cookie she took, the man took one too. This was infuriating her but she didn't want to cause a scene. When only one cookie remained, she thought: "ah...What will this abusive man do now?" Then, the man, taking the last cookie, divided it into half, giving her one half. Ah! That was too much! She was much too angry now! In a huff, she took her book, her things and stormed to the boarding place. When she sat down in her seat, inside the plane, she looked into her purse to take her eyeglasses, and, to her surprise, her packet of cookies were there, untouched, unopened! She felt so ashamed! She realized that she was wrong. She had forgotten that her cookies were kept in her purse. The man had divided his cookies with her, without feeling angry or bitter...while she had been very angry, thinking that she was dividing her cookies with him. And now there was no chance to explain herself...or to apologize.

There are 4 things that you cannot recover:
- The stone after the throw.
- The word after it's said.
- The occasion after the loss.
- The time after it's gone.

(Coach Clayton McCullah) "Real men are humble...Real men have no reason to boast. Their confidence is inward and doesn't need the approval of the world. Status, how much money you make... all that stuff fades with time. They have an understanding of where they fit into the bigger picture of life and do not see themselves as greater than they really are."

No one likes a braggart. Sometimes people even boast about how humble they are! A truly humble man does things without needing attention or praise, but because it is the right thing to do. I find it amusing when someone does an act of kindness for someone else without letting them know it was them that did the act and yet they turn around and tell others what they did. Although it feels nice to be recognized for the hard work or great efforts we have done, the only one we need to please is God.

Once there was a boy who had anger and jealousy in him. He turned it on one of his friends and treated him harshly. This friend did not understand what he had done wrong. For several months the friend endured the unkind remarks and hostility this boy directed at him.

One day the boy was running a race and was badly hurt. He was able to finish the race by sheer determination. Afterward he sat by the side of the road waiting for someone to come and help him. Several people passed him by without noticing his trouble. Finally, the young man he had been harassing came along and noticed he was hurt. This young man had also been running in the race and was quite hot and tired. But without complaint and knowing how much the boy disliked him, the young man picked him up and carried him to get the help he needed. The boy received much praise over the fact that he finished the race while hurt. Not a word was mentioned about the young man who helped him by either the boy or the young man himself. The young man had done what was right and humbled himself to help a friend. This act of humility touched the hardened heart of his friend and restored their friendship.

(Barry Farr) "I guess honesty is an aspect of humility. Humility is not weakness rather it is strength under control. One of my favorite stories of Jesus is the time in the garden right before His crucifixion when the soldiers came to arrest Him. Judas led a detachment of soldiers to arrest Jesus and when they actually came close to Him, He asked them who they were looking for. They told Him Jesus of Nazareth and He responded, that's Me. When He told them who He was they drew back and fell to the ground (John 18:4-6). Yes, they fell to the ground! Jesus had such power that just by speaking they fell to the ground in fear, but He did not use the power He had available to Him; that my friend is humility! As the story continues it becomes even clearer. One of Jesus' friends drew his sword and cut off the ear of one of the persons who had come to arrest Jesus. Jesus stopped them all and told his friend don't you understand that if I wanted to I could ask my Father to send twelve detachments of angels to rescue Me? He did not have to suffer and die, He chose to for you and me – that my friend is humility (Matthew 26:50-54).

The greatest example of humbleness is in Jesus. The Son of God left His throne in heaven to take on all our sins. He was perfect and blameless yet He walked with sinners.
John 13:1-17 gives an amazing example of just how humble Jesus is.

"Just before the Passover Feast, Jesus knew that the time had come to leave this world to go the Father. Having loved his dear companions, he continued to love them right to the end. It was suppertime. The Devil by now had Judas, son of Simon the Iscariot, firmly in his grip, all set for the betrayal.

Jesus knew that the Father had put him in complete charge of everything; that he came from God and was on his way back to God. So he got up from the supper table, set aside his robe, and put on an apron. Then he poured water into a basin and began to wash the feet of the disciples, drying them with his apron. When he got to Simon Peter, Peter said, 'Master, you wash my feet?' Jesus answered, 'You don't understand now what I'm doing, but it will be clear enough to you later.'

Peter persisted, 'You're not going to wash my feet-ever!'

Jesus said, 'If I can't wash you, you can't be part of what I'm doing.'

'Master!' said Peter. 'Not only my feet, then. Wash my hands! Wash my head!'

Jesus said, 'If you've had a bath in the morning, you only need your feet washed now and you're clean from head to toe. My concern, you understand, is holiness, not hygiene. So now you're clean, but not every one of you.' (He knew who was betraying him. That's why he said, 'Not every one of you.') After he had finished washing their feet, he took his robe, put it back on, and went back to his place at the table.

Then he said, 'Do you understand what I have done to you? You address me as 'Teacher' and 'Master' and rightly so. That is what I am. So if I, the Master and Teacher, washed your feet, you must now wash each other's feet. I've laid down a pattern for you. What I've done, you do. I'm only pointing out the obvious. A servant is not ranked above his master; an employee doesn't give orders to the employer. If you understand what I'm telling you, act like it- and live a blessed life."

Traveling the Palestine road in the first century was very filthy. They didn't have Nikes or Speerys to wear. They wore sandals, which led to some pretty dirty feet. Whenever people would get together for a meal with family and friends it was a MUST that their feet be washed. Especially since their tables were low and their feet were evident. Jesus and his disciples were at the table and Jesus gets up and begins to wash their feet. The disciples were shocked! This was the job of the lowest of servants! "Jesus shouldn't be doing this!" they must have thought. It was an act of humility and condescension. Their Master and Lord washing their feet when it should have been them washing His. I can only imagine the looks they were giving each other as Jesus knelt before them and gently poured water over their dusty, filthy feet. But Jesus didn't come to earth the first time as a King or a Conqueror, but as a Servant. He didn't come for others to serve Him but to serve others. He came to give His life for the sake of others. This act of humbleness expressed with a towel and basin of water was a prelude of His ultimate act of humility and love when He willing hung on the cross.

What Jesus was doing was the very opposite of what His disciples had just done. You see, shortly before this event, they had been bickering with each other about which one of them was greater. At the time there was no servant around to wash their feet and it didn't apparently occur to any of them to wash each other's feet. They were speechless and stunned when Jesus Himself stooped to a task considered so low. Peter, who was never shy for words, was very uncomfortable with the situation of his Master and Lord washing his feet. He spoke up and protested: "You shall never wash my feet!"

What Jesus said next must have stunned Peter even more. "Unless I wash you, you have no part of me." Peter had a true love for Jesus and wanted to please Him, but sometimes didn't always get what was going on. This was one of those times for he then requested that Jesus wash all of him! By saying this he was trying to show his loyalty to Christ. Peter had already been cleaned of his sin through salvation and did not need to be washed again in a spiritual sense. Once you are saved in Christ you are always saved. You are saved by faith not by works or anything else. We have to be "cleaned" again as we walk through an unclean world by asking forgiveness of the sins we continue to make. Peter and the other disciples only needed this temporary cleaning.

This is just one example of many truths that Christians can use in their own lives. First, when we come and ask Christ to wash away our sins He does so completely and permanently. Nothing we can do will clean us from our sins. Only the blood Christ gave on the cross for our sins can make us clean in God's eyes again. We live in a sin infested world, and as we are walking through life we get dirty and filthy with sin and need continual cleansing. This is done by the power of the Holy Spirit who lives within us, through the "washing of water by the Word of God, given to us to equip us for every good work" (2 Timothy 3:16-17).

Also, when Jesus washed the disciples' feet, He told them (and us) "I have given you an example, that you should do as I have done to you" (John 13:15). He is telling us, as his followers, that we should imitate Him and serve each other in lowliness of heart and mind. We should build each other up in humbleness and love. God promises that true greatness in His kingdom is achieved by those with a servant's heart.

Real men are humble.

Chapter 5

FAITHFULNESS

"If you are faithful in little things, you will be faithful in large ones. But if you are dishonest in little things, you won't be honest with greater responsibilities. And if you are untrustworthy about worldly wealth, who will trust you with the true riches of heaven? And if you are not faithful with other people's things, why should you be trusted with things of your own"(Luke 16:10-12)?

(Bruce Seymour) "Integrity, Honesty and Faithfulness are three most important things. You must guard these three like it is the gold in Ft. Knox. If you stay honest (tell no lies), always treat others fairly in all situations, and stay faithful in all things it doesn't matter how successful, rich or smart you are. These things stay with you. But, if you lie, cheat, or steal even once you can never completely repair the damage."

There once was a little boy who had a bad temper. His father gave him a bag of nails and told him that every time he lost his temper, he must hammer a nail into the back of the fence. The first day the boy had driven 37 nails into the fence. Over the next few weeks, as he learned to control his anger, the number of nails hammered daily gradually dwindled down. He discovered it was easier to hold his temper than to drive those nails into the fence.

Finally, the day came when the boy didn't lose his temper at all. He told his father about it and the father suggested that the boy now pull out one nail for each day that he was able to hold his temper. The days passed and the young boy was finally able to tell his father that all the nails were gone. The father took his son by the hand and led him to the fence.

He said, 'You've done well, my son, but look at the holes in the fence. The fence will never be the same. When you say things in anger, they leave a scar just like this one. You can put a knife in a man and draw it out. It won't matter how many times you say I'm sorry, the wound is still there and a verbal wound is just as bad as a physical one.'

Your words and your actions can leave scars on others, whether it is a bad temper, lying, cheating or any other negative action. Once done, the damage is there. Sure, they can forgive you, but you have permanently scarred them.

(Kwasi Ofori-Yeboah) "Like loyalty implies dependability and reliability, you want to be known as a man of your word; someone who can be counted on to make good on his promises. That means exercising extreme caution in your decision making to ensure that you can follow through on your decisions and promises. This is very important especially in marriage. Faithfulness implies that your wife can trust you at all times and under all circumstances. Being faithful will also give you the peace of mind to live with yourself in what you do because your conscience will not be bothering you about something you did, that you know you shouldn't have done. Faithfulness has the dual benefits of keeping you at peace and your wife and friends at rest. Make it your goal to be faithful at all times and you will be glad you did."

There is a purpose to life's events, to teach you how to laugh more or not to cry too hard. You can't make someone love you, all you can do is be someone who can be loved, and the rest is up to the person to realize your worth. It's better to lose your pride to the one you love, than to lose the one you love because of pride. We spend too much time looking for the right person to love or finding fault with those we already love, when instead we should be perfecting the love we give.

(Coach Daniel Bayless) "Loyalty + Integrity = Faithfulness"

(Barry Farr) "I want to challenge you to be faithful. I know you have struggled with trusting God and I know you have had your share of disappointments because key people in your life have not been faithful, but God has given you some awesome people to fill the gap and faithfully support you in your journey. I think I have seen in you that you want to be the opposite of those who have failed you. That is not a bad thing. Remember that reacting to others failure is not enough; make it your goal to be faithful and loyal to those you love, and never choose your own comfort or success over theirs."

It's so easy to look back on our lives and see where others have let us down. But, it's much more difficult to look back and see where we have let others down. Make sure you are faithful to those you love in your life. Be there for them when they need you. Encourage them when encouragement is needed. Praise them for the good you see in their lives. Let your faithfulness be a source of strength to those who know you.

Ernest Hemingway said, "What is moral is what you feel good after, and what is immoral is what your feel bad after."

Real men are faithful

Michael, Bryce, Brandon and Tyler

Chapter 6

GRATEFULNESS

"Be thankful in all circumstances, for this is God's will for you who belong to Christ Jesus" (1 Thessalonians 5:18).

(Coach Daniel Bayless) "When you feel grateful, express it."

Jake's Story

Sometimes God brings the most interesting people into your life. I met "Jake" through my daughter Bailey. "Jake" is one of these guys you just can't help but smile when you hear his name. He has the most unusual sense of humor and a witty intellect to go along with it. When I first met "Jake" I just thought he was this quirky young man who was always cracking jokes and smiling. Over time I realized he has a heart of gold and can be considered a loyal friend. Someone you can count on when you need him. Something about "Jake" that a lot of people don't understand though is that he covers his hurt with humor. Another thing people might not be aware of is "Jake" is grateful for the people he cherishes in his life. The following is an essay he wrote in school. A real man is grateful.

A situation that not only terrifies me but, undoubtedly, many other individuals is the thought of loneliness. The Oxford Dictionary defines loneliness as a "sadness because one has no friends or company," but it is much larger than they describe. Loneliness is a sickness that seeps through the cracks of reality and darkens the soul to its extinction. Loneliness acts as a monarch and uses depression, despair, pain, and agony to tighten its grip on the individual. Loneliness is not kind, and will not pity any single group of individuals. It has fortified its grip in children, young adults, women, and men from every race, ethnic group, and country. Loneliness, simply put, has one goal and that is to make its victim feel alienated from the world. Once that happens the person is 100 percent at risk to succumb to loneliness's bleak outlook on their life. Even though loneliness is the fright I have struggled the most with, knowing why it scares me has helped make it a more bearable subject.

Loneliness was most prevalent for me during my childhood. I had two parents that got up, got ready, and went to work before I was even awake. I spent most mornings in silence within my empty house: forcing myself to shower, pick out my clothes, cook breakfast, make my bed, pack my school supplies, and catch the bus. At school, if I didn't spend at least one visit in the office a day then it wasn't a regular school day for me. In class I acted up the majority of the time because it allowed me to get the entire class to pay attention to me. This was an important feeling to me because it was an experience that I couldn't get at home and eventually, it turned me into the class clown because I was striving to entertain them so I could get their approval. After school neither one of my parents ever made it home before 8 o'clock and I didn't have any friends outside of a modest few from school; so I spent a lot of my free time alone. Each day, after school let out, I always took the bus home and went straight to sleep. However, a kid can only sleep so much before the body begins to reject it and they no longer can. So to shave a few hours off my day I began to eat constantly, and consequently I started gaining weight by the pounds. When my parents were home though, they spent every waking minute with me slamming doors, launching valuables across the room, complaining about their jobs, or leaving because neither one would want to argue with the other any longer.

Isaac Newton's third law explains,"for every action, there is an equal and opposite reaction," which means for everything that has happened to me in my past, it will affect me some way in the future. When I went to primary school, I was always acting up, which meant I was never in class to learn the criteria. Since my parents were never home they couldn't tutor me through my assignments and subsequently my grades fell out from beneath themselves. The time I didn't spend at school I spent sitting alone at home. I used eating as a recreational pastime and in the aftermath my body picked up a substantial amount of weight. With all the weight that I had gained, added on to the fact that I was predominantly surrounded by kids my own age, I began to be ridiculed by the other students. Being an object of everyone's taunting meant that finding a genuine friend was all but impossible. My social skills were lacking and probably all but absent without any friends or family that I could have conversations with. This caused me to never speak up about my ideas, solutions, and beliefs with anyone including: my classmates, teachers, or loved ones. Without sociality I developed a habit of talking to myself to compensate for the despair of seclusion I felt. Consequently, all of these things greatly lowered my self-esteem and made me feel like I wasn't good enough to compete with any of the other kids in my class or in my age group. So at an early age I refused to compete in sports for fear of the other players ridiculing me for my lack of athletic ability and I abandoned homework because I believed that I was never going to catch up to the other students. With all of these problems piling up I began to become increasingly depressed and developed sickness more often than I ever encountered before. Finally, loneliness had dragged me to my lowest point and I contemplated suicide as an escape to all my problems.

All of these things have built up, adding to my fear of loneliness, and have had an effect on me somewhere in my life. Whether it be right away or 10 years down the road this fear has ranged from stopping me from asking the beautiful girl out for the school dance, to being so clinically depressed that I don't want to meet another human being, because the thought of telling them goodbye is too much. Loneliness reminds me every day what kind of life I don't want to return to each time I reflect on it, and this is a fear that has the possibility of never truly disappearing. Loneliness has affected me in many ways and repairing the rampant scars that it mercilessly left behind, beneath my skin, has been a vigorous effort. However, just like any scar, loneliness will never truly leave and in all likelihood it will have a say in every future action I take.

Although loneliness was a painful part of "Jake's" past it is also one of the reason's he honestly cherishes the people in his life and is loyal to those he cares greatly about. Loyalty and gratefulness are rare traits in anyone. A real man shows both.

Count your blessings every day. When you think you don't have something to be thankful for start listing things and you will be surprised. Are you in good health? Do you have a job? Did you wake up? Did you sleep in a warm bed? Did you have food to eat? There are always things to be grateful for. The first one you should always do daily is to express your gratefulness to God.

If someone has given you something or bought you something the very first thing out of your mouth should be thank you! Under no circumstance should you complain about what they have done for you. They did not have to do it. When you complain you will make others feel like what they are doing is not appreciated. After a while, people will think there is no pleasing you so what's the point in doing or giving to you. Plus it's just good manners.

(Griff Schoen) "Be thankful for all you have and be content in your circumstances. Don't try to keep up with the Joneses. With gratefulness comes humility. Treat others as if they are better than you, but don't become a doormat either. Learn when to stand up for yourself but when you do, be respectful."

Keeping up with the Jones' means you always want what someone else has. That's called coveting and it's a sin. Be grateful that you have what you have and don't look at someone else's life and want their "things." Before you know it you will be in debt up to your eyeballs trying to keep up with them which will lead to stress. Ask someone who has lost everything and had to start over what they are grateful for.

(Papa & Granny) "Above everything always be grateful for the small or big things people have done or will do for you."

If you are always taking and never giving you need to stop. You're taking advantage of someone. If someone is doing something out of the kindness of their heart for you, make sure you are returning the kindness. It doesn't have to involve money. Maybe it involves your time or your work. One way of showing gratefulness is by gladly doing something that needs to be done without complaint and possibly without even being asked to do it. There are ways both big and small that you can show gratitude for things people have done for you both big and small. Look for these things and do them.

(Barry Farr) "I want to encourage you to remember that being grateful can have amazing power. When you and I are grateful, or thankful it changes our perspective. It may not change our circumstances, but it will change how we view our circumstances and how we respond to our circumstance. I have sorrow and pain every day because I wish Jordan was still here, but I am filled with gratefulness and thanksgiving when I think of the 17 years God allowed me to enjoy with him. I miss him, but I am grateful that I have confidence that Jordan is with the Lord and nothing, not even the sum of everything I could think of that he might have enjoyed in this life were he to live here until he was 117 can compare with what he already has...I do not think you have to be grateful or thankful for the bad things that have happened but you can and should be thankful and grateful for the wonderful things that have come into your life as a result of the junk that happened to you."

- Be thankful when you don't know something...for it gives you the opportunity to learn.

- Be thankful for the difficult times...during those times you grow.

- Be thankful for your limitations...they give you opportunities for improvement.

- Be thankful for each new challenge...which will build your strength and character.

- Be thankful for your mistakes...they will teach you a valuable lesson.

- Be thankful when you're tired and weary...yet, a life of rich fulfillment comes to those who are thankful for the setbacks.

- Gratitude can turn a negative into a positive...find a way to be thankful for your troubles and they can become your blessings.

Real men are grateful.

Sean and Maddi

Chapter 7

WISDOM

"In the same way, wisdom is sweet to your soul. If you find it, you will have a bright future, and your hopes will not be cut short" (Proverbs 24:14).

(Coach Daniel Bayless) "I can't let myself give all this advice without sharing where my strength comes from. I don't know how a man can measure up to what I have talked about without a personal relationship with Jesus Christ."

Sean's Story

A Father's Absence of Love

It's impossible to anticipate the family struggles and turmoil that will be encountered as a young boy grows into a man. As a child you want to receive love and affection from your parents, but not everyone receives those emotions. My father was an abusive alcoholic, manipulative, and a pathological liar. The mental abuse was the most detrimental as he was always discouraging, insulting, and belittling his family. My father slapped my brother across the face at a public swimming pool busting his lip open because he misbehaved; he broke furniture and forced my mother to clean it up, and lifted me off the ground by my head and threw me to the ground. After a while I started to think maybe there was something wrong with me, but I was just trying to make excuses for the man I so desperately wanted to have a loving relationship with. Over time, my relationship with my father deteriorated and became nonexistent. Then my parents divorced and my mother raised me at the age of twelve on. As time went on I built a wall of resentment towards my father and I developed an anger reservoir that would be still one minute but flood the next. I would verbally lash out toward my mother and brother, saying hurtful things at times, just as my father use to. It was an emotion that was hard to control because of the hate that had developed inside of me for a father that treated me with no sign of remorse. The man I loathed and despised for the years of damage he inflicted on my family was starting to surface in my behavior towards others.

"Because human anger does not produce the righteousness that God desires." (James 1:20).

I eventually understood the adverse effects my father's violence had caused and made the decision to change my behavior, overcome my aggression, and become a man of integrity while treating others respectfully. Forgiveness, on the other hand, was a struggle for me. Although, I had changed to become a better person I was still holding on to the hate for my father, which prevented me from forgiving him. It was only after reading a Christian novel called The Shack that I realized the unnecessary burden I had been carrying for the past 10 years. I finally gave my pain to God by forgiving my father, for when you give your problems and worries to God, He fills your heart with love while renewing His purpose within you. It was a weight off my shoulders not having to carry that around anymore and although I forgave my father, I will never forget what he did.

"For if you forgive other people when they sin against you, your heavenly Father will also forgive you. But if you do not forgive others their sins, your Father will not forgive you sins" (Matthew 6:14-15).

Negative experiences in life can crumble away your resolve and affect the outcome of your development as a man. You have to summon the strength to persevere in life and not let the difficulties encountered in the past prevent you from developing into the person God made you to be. You have to decide for yourself the type of man you desire to be despite your struggles. I didn't realize until years later, far removed from the abuse of my father, that my suffering and will to overcome such an obstacle shaped my character as a man.

"Not only that, but we rejoice in our sufferings, knowing that suffering produces endurance, and endurance produces character, and character produces hope, and hope does not put us to shame, because God's love has been poured into our hearts through the Holy Spirit who has been given to us" (Romans 5:3-5).

If I did not suffer the abuse from my father while also, witnessing the pain he inflicted on my family I would almost certainly not have the strong inclination today to become the most loving, nurturing father and husband I can be. Sometimes I think, "What would it have been like to have a father who loved and cared about me?"A father who would offer advice, one who would support my involvement in various activities, and provide much needed guidance through my journey to manhood." Although I wish my father had a more prominent role in my life growing up, I'm more than happy with the person I've become. I owe much gratitude to my mother for helping instill the moral values and beliefs that I carry with me today; a woman who quickly made sacrifices to ensure the betterment of her family while taking on the added responsibilities necessary when no father figure is present. I have become strong and accomplished many things. I graduated summa cum laude with a Bachelor's degree in Marketing Management, pursued a MBA, have a financially rewarding career, and a beautiful fiancé` that has helped renew my faith in Christ. It was through her that God touched and changed my life and for that I will be forever thankful.

"He gives power to the paint, and to him who has no might he increases strength. Even youths shall faint and be weary, and young men shall fall exhausted; but they who wait for the Lord shall renew their strength; they shall mount up with wings like eagles; they shall run and not be weary; they shall walk and not faint" (Isaiah 40:29-31).

There is one particular quote written by Corrie Ten Boom that helps me put everything into perspective. He states, "Every experience God gives us, every person He puts in our lives is the perfect preparation for the future that only He can see." It's about leaning in and fully trusting in the Lord. Give your problems up to Him with complete faith and He will provide the road for you to follow. Always remember, you decide the Man you want to be. Sure there might be negative influences that seem overwhelming at times but you are the one that decides if it will affect your behavior and alter the character that you have been striving to maintain. We all have different paths but the road traveled is the same through Christ.

If you haven't accepted Christ, and begun a personal relationship with God by studying His word, praying, and attending a church then you are already behind in this game of life and you are on the losing end.

Your life will consist of many ups and downs. God tells us in 2 Corinthians 12:9-10 that He is strong in our weakness. When we go through hard times it's our faith that God is holding us in His hands and He is faithful to us above anyone else that will pull us through.

(Kwasi Ofori-Yeboah) "We are down to the most important of all topics of life – a relationship with God. Like most young people, I had a lot of questions at that age and frankly did not want to be bothered by the 'God question.' However, I had to be true to myself and confront some of the questions that pop up in our minds every so often; why am I here? Where did I come from? What is this life all about? And where do I go from here? We all have to answer these questions as we contemplate life and its meaning. These questions won't go away no matter how hard we try to ignore them or sweep them under the rug, so we have to confront them.

One way is to provide our own answers which are inadequate, and we must be humble enough to recognize the limitations of our answers. We must then look of the answers somewhere else. But where does one begin? I thought to myself, surely life could have come about by accident not by chance. But the more I thought about it, the less that position made sense. Something that comes about by random happenings will not be so organized and so precise. Take the sun rise and sun set and the seasons and the harmony in nature and they all point to one fact; something or somebody must have had a hand in this.

Reason dictates that we must give credit where credit is due. And when one steps back to observe nature and life in general, there is no reasonable conclusion other than an author or a creator is responsible for such a masterpiece.

Yes, there is a lot of evil in this world and how do we explain that in the face of a good God being the creator of this world? A valid question deserves a thorough answer but time and space elude me here.

The next question though is what if anything at all, has this Creator got to do with me? My first thought was nothing! But as I pondered the question further, it dawned on me that, the correct response is everything. How do I know that? As I wondered about life and who could be behind it and its sustenance, and as I secretly longed for answers to these questions, I started paying attention to what my parents had been saying to me since childhood, and that is, to have a meaningful relationship with God. I didn't know how, and wasn't even sure if I wanted to. But one day during a gospel concert, the leader of the band, after a brief sermon, issued a call to anyone who wanted to accept Jesus as Lord and savior to repeat a prayer of salvation after him. I just closed my eyes and waited for him to complete the prayer so I could go home. But, as I bowed my head in prayer, I felt a strong urge to heed his call to repentance. However, I had an objection. I just didn't think I could follow God. I mean all the dos and don'ts of Christianity were too much, I thought. But then a passage of the Bible came to mind, 'with God all things are possible' (Matthew 19:26). This passage rung in my head several times after which I said, OK, God, if all things are possible with you, then I am going to turn my life to you and please make it possible for me to walk with You and live for You.

After that I heeded the leader's call and turned my life over to God by repenting of my sins and inviting Jesus into my life. I have shied away from quoting a lot of Bible verses to make my point, but I can assure you that the emptiness that we all feel can only be filled with a fellowship and a relationship with God.

A lot of the questions on our minds are answered in the Bible. We are here for a reason, and while we may not get all the answers to all our questions, we shouldn't resist the call of God. Or we shouldn't wait till we have all our questions answered. If we will be humble enough to see God, I can assure you that in His own way, He will reveal Himself to us. He desires to fellowship with us because He created us and wants us to be with Him. However, we can turn Him off by occupying ourselves and staying busy with the activities of life.

I know God wants a relationship with each of us not based on my experience only, but as you have experienced yourself, He talks to you when you are by yourself. When you lie in bed and wonder about life, He makes His presence felt. All you need to do is to answer His call and leave the rest to Him. He is not going to force us to accept Him. But we will have no excuse for not accepting Him, knowing fully well in our hearts that yes, He did answer a prayer (that we didn't even say out loud), that yes, He did answer some of the questions on our mind, and yes, He did stir our hearts. In short, we all have personal experiences directing us to the power and the presence of God, the question is how we would respond? I'd say, give God a chance. We could all use His help and not because we can't work hard to make enough to pay our bills. But because, when all is said and done, our journey here is going to come to an end, then what? We have limited control in this world and God has offered to help us along the way.

We should take advantage of His offer. He will help us to have integrity, honesty, loyalty, humility, and industriousness. He will give you wisdom and guide you in college and career choices. He will help you find a soul mate. He will be a better companion than you can find elsewhere because He will never fail you. There will be hard times, but He will be there to see you through them. Like a ship tossed about on rough waters, He will be your compass and your anchor when you come to shore.

Without Him though, this ship will be tossed about and wind up in an undesirable location. Give Him a chance, let Him be your captain and no matter how high the tides, and how choppy the waters, you will make a safe landing."

(Stephanie Schraeder) "And for everyone you meet, you don't know what is going on in their lives; you may be the only smiling face they see that day. Live well, laugh often, and love much. And always know that you are also loved beyond measure. 'For God so love YOU, that He gave His only begotten Son so that whosoever believes in Him will not perish but have everlasting life!'"

You are loved. You are loved so much that God Himself, the creator of EVERYTHING sent his one and only son to come to earth and die just so we could someday spend eternity in Heaven with Him. Live a life that is pleasing to Him not heartbreaking. Live a life that will draw others into a relationship with Him and someday when you stand face to face He will say to you, "well done my good and faithful servant."

(Coach Robby Hoegh) "At the end of this life we answer to one person, and that is the God of this universe. Having a relationship with Christ and living with a Kingdom purpose is going to continue to get more difficult in the world we live. Draw close to the Word, and God will reveal himself to you, and what He does with your life will be a thing of beauty."

This world is a messed up place. More and more people are turning away from the way of life God has told us to live in order to live a self-pleasing life-style. But one day we will all stand before Him and answer for the type of life we lived.

In everything you do, do so in a manner that will please Him. Being a Christian does not mean attending church every week. It's a way of life. It means following how Christ lived, treating others how Christ did.

(Papa & Granny) "Pray about giving your life to Jesus. Without Him to guide you in your life you can make some big mistakes. Just ask Him to guide you day by day in everything you do."

Of all the decisions you will make in your life, giving your life completely to God will be the biggest and by far the best decision you will ever make! This home on Earth is just temporary. We are only meant to be here a very brief amount of time. Our real home is in Heaven. God has a place all planned out just waiting for our arrival. As much as we love our friends and our family we should love our God even more so and our lives here on this Earth should reflect that more than anything else. He should come first above all else. At the end of this life it will be His arms we fall into and His voice that will say, "Welcome home, I've been waiting for you."

Chapter 8

LOVE

"If I speak with human eloquence and angelic ecstasy but don't have love, I'm nothing but the creaking of a rusty gate. If I speak God's Word with power, revealing all his mysteries and making everything plain as day, and if I have faith that says to a mountain, 'Jump,' and it jumps, but I don't love, I'm nothing. If I give everything I own to the poor and even go to the stake to be burned as a martyr, but I don't love, I've gotten nowhere. So, no matter what I say, what I believe, and what I do, I'm bankrupt without love...

A special story about a boy named David.

In a land where there was not much beauty, an Angel was sent down from heaven to bring happiness and love to the people living there. The Angel took on the mortal name of Madison while on Earth. She was beautiful to look upon although some mere mortals could not see her beauty. Her heart was pure, true, and tender, filled with goodness and kindness. She was a very shy Angel though, always doubting herself. She did not know that people on earth could be so cruel and hurtful to each other at times and it broke her heart.

One day Maddi (The Angel's friends bestowed her with this very special name) came home from a place she said was evil and bad, a place with a wicked name of SCHOOL! The mere sound of it sent shivers up Maddi's spine!

Upon entering her lovely home she observed her earthly mother cooking supper. Maddi sat down with her mother and began telling her about this young man who was new to the place of torture, school. This boy scared Maddi. As she told her mom about him her big blue eyes grew wider and wider. She said he was different. He had been in battles in a far away land and had scars to show of the fights he had fought. He told of a gang he belonged to that frightened Maddi much. Maddi believed this young warrior was full of darkness and she did not want anything to do with him. She told of how he dressed in the dark attire of his old ways. Then, she bestowed the name of Vampire Boy upon him and Maddi and all her friend called him that name. All of Maddi's friends were also scared of Vampire Boy. They did not know him or understand his life.

One day, while being silly with her friends, they called Vampire Boy and listened to his voice message on his phone. The other girls just laughed and giggled like girls will do. Mortal girls are strange that way. But Maddi returned to her home disturbed. She sought out her mother for wisdom. Maddi wanted her mother to hear Vampire Boy's voice so she called and listened. Her mother did not understand what was upsetting Maddi so much at first. After she listened to the message, Maddi told her mother she thought he sounded so sad and it hurt her somehow and she didn't understand it. Because her mother was not an Angel like Maddi she did not know what she was feeling so she hugged her and let her go on her way.

A few nights later, Maddi was doing something a lot of mortals like to do, she was on her computer. Maddi discovered something that twisted her heart and made it hurt. She called her mother over. Her mother discovered Maddi sitting staring at the computer at Vampire Boys MySpace page with tears sliding down her face. Maddi turned and said to her mother, "Mom, it breaks my heart, he seems so sad. His name on here is Lonely Boy and he wrote beside it how the world is a cold, lonely place and he has hurt people and maybe he should just go away." This had Maddi so upset. Her soft pure heart could not handle the thought of someone being that sad. Her mother told Maddi that maybe she should tell him how it bothered her. Now, her mother didn't really believe Maddie would say anything to this boy because Maddi did not like talking to any boys. She believed them to be cruel and hurtful. But apparently Maddi found the courage to tell this young man and the next time she talked to her mother she told her he had changed some of the things on his page after she talked to him. This made Maddi so happy! All of a sudden she was no longer calling him Vampire Boy and she was jumping all over anyone who called him that! She felt so ashamed of herself for calling him that in the first place. It had become one of her biggest regrets and she hoped he would forgive her. Instead, she started referring to him by his given name of David. A strong name after a great King in the Bible who killed a giant and God referred to as, "A man after my own heart."

Maddi told her mother she wanted David to be really happy. She wanted her mother to meet David. She believed he was nice and wanted her other friends to like him instead of being scared. She thought if her mother liked him and thought he was good then the rest would chill about her wanting to be friends with him. It's hard sometimes for mortals to understand the hearts of Angels. So her mother met him and discovered a very intelligent, kind young man.

Now in Maddi's world things were looking happier. David and Maddi were talking all the time and that made her angel face glow! The two of them were slowly becoming very special friends. So opposite from each other, but somehow drawn together. David brought out courage in Maddi she did not have before and Maddi taught David about the unconditional love of a friend.

Maddi had to fight many word wars with other kids over her friendship with David, but she stood her ground and did not care what others said. They tried to pierce her heart and bring her down but they did not realize Angels have extraordinary power and are hard to bring down.

Although Maddi and David eventually moved to different lands their friendship bond was still strong and loyal.

"If I could speak all the languages of earth and of angels, but didn't love others, I would only be a noisy clanging cymbal. If I had the gift of prophecy, and if I understood all of God's secret plans and possessed all knowledge, and if I had such faith that I could move mountains, but didn't love others, I would be nothing. If I gave everything I have to the poor and even sacrificed my body, I could boast about it, but if I didn't love others, I would have gained nothing. Love is patient and kind. Love is not jealous or boastful or proud or rude. It does not demand its own way. It is not irritable, and it keeps no recourse of being wronged. It does not rejoice about injustice but rejoices whenever the truth wins out. Love never gives up, never loses faith, is always hopeful, and endures through every circumstance. Love will last forever. All that I know now is partial and incomplete, but then I will know everything completely, just as God now knows me completely. Three things will last forever ~faith, hope, and love~and the greatest of these is love" (1 Corinthians 13).

David was a 13-year-old boy who moved to our town from Texas. He looked different and acted different than what the kids there were use to being around. His life there was harsh. Surrounded by gangs and violence, it was a frightening place for him to grow up. When he moved to our small town in Kansas he was a fish out of water. Rumors about him floated all over town. My daughter, Madison, had the courage to extend a hand of friendship. This small action had a big impact on David's life. He started attending youth group and eventually accepted Christ as his Savior.

David is living back in Texas now and is doing well. When I recently asked him what his definition of a real man was this was his response:

"In my definition a man should be firm, should show respect to everyone even when they don't deserve it. He should take care of his business without involving the world. A man should admit when he's wrong whenever he is. A man should keep his word as much as possible and shouldn't make thousands of excuses for himself. If he is a father he should try to spend time with his kids and discipline them in love whenever they are wrong. A man should be accepting with an unconditional amount of love and teach his kids right from wrong."

One small act of love can change a life. A real man appreciates love when it is shown to him and in return shows love to others.

Love is a word that gets casually tossed around without truly understanding its power. Know and understand what love is. It's more than just an emotional feeling, it's a purpose. You will save yourself and the people in your life a lot of heartache if you can understand what real love is.

(Paul Dillman) "When I met Beth she showed me how to show and express love to my children and others. In our marriage, the areas I felt I was lacking, she has helped me to be more affectionate with my children, and show and tell expressions of love to them. Learning from mistakes I make in life and changing my ways have led to accomplishments and make me feel better about myself."

"Love never gives up..."

Love is more than just a few stages. It's what keeps

you from giving up; it's what pulls you through hard times. There are people who are in love with the IDEA of being in love, but that isn't love itself, that is a fantasy. Love is about commitment and loyalty and faithfulness.

People are going to let you down. Their human just like you, and they have faults. Part of loving someone is forgiving them when they let you down. It's not always easy, but if you have a sincere love for them, it is something you must practice. I once heard a preacher say, "What has someone done to you that is SO bad that you can't forgive them, yet YOUR sins put the nails in Christ's hands and He forgave you."

If you love someone, they should know it. Tell them often! Don't be afraid to overuse the phrase, "I love you." it never gets too old to hear. Don't just tell them, but show them with your patients towards them. Nobody is perfect. Sometimes you just have to get over yourself and show love.

(Coach Clayton McCullah) "Real men Love others...Sacrificially. They put others needs before their own. They are chivalrous and conduct themselves with honor towards others. Real men are kind to others. They see the value in everyone. Everyone...no matter who they are has value. They all start out as a child full of wonder and curiosity. They are able to see that understanding our world and its circumstances can change people. Nevertheless, real men are able to see past it. They stand up for the weak, they defend the honor of those less fortunate. Anyone can be mean, but a man will look out for the down trodden; those hurting, and will treat them as though they are important, and a real man will see the value and importance in doing so."

"Love cares more for others more than for self..."

The definition of sacrifice is giving up of something highly valued for the sake of one considered too have a greater value or claim. The Bible tells us we are to humble ourselves and consider others above us. One of the best feelings in the world is when you are able to help someone else. There are a lot of hurting people in this world. Open your eyes and see what is going on around you and ask yourself, "What can I do to help?" Have a radical love for others!

I attended church my entire life. I became a Christian when I was in fourth grade. I grew up hearing all the Bible stories and going to church camps, singing hymns and worship songs.

It wasn't until I was in my late thirties that I finally stopped "playing church," and started living the love Christ demonstrated for me. I was sitting in church, and as much as I hate to admit this, not really listening to what the preacher was saying. All of a sudden, it was like God thumped me upside the head! Out of nowhere this thought was in my mind, "You need to minister to youth." I had worked with youth before, teaching Sunday school mainly. But I knew this time was different. God didn't want me to just teach them in a classroom setting where most of them would barely attend. He wanted me to go out and live His love toward them. He wanted me to reach out to the kids most people would not even talk to.

So my ministry began. I started leading the very small youth group at our church. I believe at that time it consisted of four youth (two of which were my own daughters). I challenged them to talk to kids they didn't normally talk to...the amazing part was...they did it!

During the next three years, I opened up my home for kids to hang out at. My front yard turned into a football, baseball, basketball, I think possibly golf maybe type field. I cooked breakfast, I cooked lunch, I cooked supper, and I cooked Monster Cookies for any youth. I discovered many of these youth never got a home cooked meal, where the family sat at the table together. I gave rides to and from school and church. Eventually, God grew that little youth group of four into an amazing, exciting, family of youth, consisting of twenty-four members of some of the roughest kids in town. At one point, when I would go into the local grocery store, one of the girls that worked there was apparently a bit ticked at me for taking her party crowd away and would show her displeasure by rolling her eyes at me and loudly announcing, "Oh look, it's that F*ing Martin woman." I always made sure I went through her lane and smiled sweetly and spoke kindly. On occasion I would leave a tip with the manager to give to her anonymously. She never attended youth group while I was there, but I heard, when we moved, she graced the doors of that church and was welcomed.

One of the most memorable moments was when the Principle of the high school called me and told me one of the boys that had started coming to my youth group was arriving very early to school every morning in order to wash and clean himself up. You see, he was living in some pretty nasty home conditions, and his mom smoked. He was embarrassed by how he smelled, and some of the kids were making fun of him. The Principle asked if I could help him out in any way. What I call my big, dumb, often gets me in trouble, soft, compassionate heart just melted. So I told my youth group that I was planning on cooking breakfast for everyone and to invite this particular boy.

He didn't drive so I had to go pick him up the next morning at six. I brought him back to my house. There was plenty of time remaining before other kids would arrive and my own children were busy getting ready for school. I made a bold step and told the boy if he would like to shower and get cleaned up for school at my house, he was more than welcome to. At first he hesitated, and gave me a look as if to say, "Who is this crazy lady?" But he accepted my offer. For the remainder of the school year, I picked him up every morning, fed him breakfast with my kids and made sure he had clean clothes to wear.

What did I sacrifice? I gave up my time, a little bit of food, a bottle of shampoo and body wash, and some detergent. What was gained? A young man, who was angry at the world, and thought nobody cared about him, and God sure didn't care, got to see what real love is. Whenever he would ask me why I did all this for him I would say, "Because God said to love others and because you are too skinny!"

Now I can't say that over the years my ministry hasn't cost me more than I wanted. There have been times when I thought the sacrifice wasn't worth it; when I felt unappreciated and taken advantage of. When I knew other people were talking about me behind my back, without understanding why I would associate with "those" kind of kids. There were times when even my family struggled to understand, when my heart would get broken over and over again. During those times, God reminded me to love anyway. I've had to learn to listen to Him and not others who are not always listening to Him. I've had to learn what unconditional love is about. It's hard. I didn't always do things perfectly. Anyone who really knows me knows I'm beautifully flawed. But I can tell you this; I have experienced so many blessings. One thing I know for sure is that my children and my close friends now know what ministering and loving someone really looks like.

Sure, life would have been much easier if I had just

stayed in my little box with just my family and close friends surrounding me, attending church for a couple hours a week. I could have been the stay-at-home-eating-chocolates-watching Ellen-life is easy kind of woman. But instead, I loved.

You can't claim to love someone and never sacrifice yourself for them. If you are always getting what you want, and never thinking of others, then you do not love. Don't tell someone, whether they are a friend, family member or spouse, that you love them, if you are not willing to put their needs before your own needs. If you are doing things you know will hurt them, stop doing them. That's love. If you are not doing something for them that you know would help them, do it. That's love.

Everyone has value in them. No one is considered better than someone else. God created us all in His image. When you judge someone, who is different than you, then you are basically criticizing God's own creation. We are all masterpieces; pieced together by the Master. He showed love to ALL of us by sacrificing His son. We don't always know what people are struggling with and what their life story is. That's why we need to show them love. It's the greatest commandment God gave. He didn't just suggest you love people who are pleasant and kind to you. He COMMANDED that you love others. Matthew 22:36-40 says, "Teacher, which is the greatest commandment in the Law?" Jesus replied, "Love the Lord your God with all your heart and with all your soul and with your entire mind. This is the first and greatest commandment. And the second is like it; 'Love your neighbor as yourself.' All the Law and the Prophets hang on these two commandments.

To even begin to understand what real love is, you must know God's love. His is a perfect love. If you don't know His love, there is no way you could possibly understand real sacrificial love. The previous scripture says to love God with every part of you. Love Him with your heart. Give Him your passions in life. Be passionate for Him. Love Him with your soul. Put Him above everything in your life. Long to know Him more. Love Him with your mind. Make your thoughts pleasing to Him. Once you do this, then it says to love others as you love yourself.

Everyone should love themselves and want the best for themselves. If you can't love others this way, then maybe you should take a look at why you don't love yourself.

One of my favorite songs is by the sing group, For King and Country, it is called, *Proof of Your Love*. The Chorus and one verse speak to me of real love.

> "*So let my life be the proof,*
>
> *the proof of your love.*
>
> *Let my love look like you*
>
> *and what you're made of.*
>
> *How you lived, how you died.*
>
> *Love is sacrifice.*
>
> *So let my life be the proof,*
>
> *the proof of your live.*
>
> *If I give to a needy soul*
>
> *but don't have love*
>
> *then who is poor?*
>
> *It seems all the poverty*
>
> *is found in me.*
>
> *When it's all said and done,*
>
> *When we sing our final song,*
>
> *Only love remains.*

(Kwasi Ofori-Yeboah) "There are different types of love. The love you feel for your friends is different from the one you feel for your family, and that is also different from the one you feel for your spouse, etc. Love is also one of those words that are easily bandied about so much so that it is easy to lose sight of its importance. So many people use it without meaning it or without understanding its meaning. By nature we are love driven. By that I mean it is part of our genetic make-up to admire and be attracted to some people and things. And there is nothing wrong in falling in love with someone. Granted, they may not feel the same way towards you, but that still doesn't diminish your natural attraction to the person. What you want to avoid is being so blinded by "love" (better called infatuation) that you throw all caution to the wind and insist on pursuing that object of your affection at all cost. You will be setting yourself up for disappointment with that kind of attitude. First Corinthians chapter 13 has a beautiful description of love that I hope you will familiarize yourself with. Of all the descriptions and definitions of love out there, none comes remotely close to capturing the true meaning of the word than you can find in this passage and that is why I highly recommend it to you. There would be less heartaches and headaches in our world if we built our relationships and families on the love described in 1 Corinthians 13. Don't be afraid to love and don't be afraid to show it. It is a sign of maturity and emotional security and not of weakness. True men love their own wives, kids, family and friends."

"Love doesn't want what it doesn't have..."

There are different types of love, but they all have strength in them:

- *Agapē* love is selfless, sacrificial, unconditional love, the highest of all loves.

- *Storge* is a love that is felt among family. It is the bond among mothers, fathers, sister and brothers.

- *Eros* is passionate love. This kind of love however does not have to be sexual. It can also be a love for someone whom you love deeper than friendship. Plato claimed Eros love is when you see the beauty inside of someone.

- *Philia* means friendship in modern Greek. It is a love that includes loyalty to friends, family, and neighbors. It requires virtue, equality and familiarity.

These are the basic Greek forms of love. But, there are three other kinds of love that I believe we tend to relate more to:

- The "IF kind of love" says, "I will love you IF you do things my way, IF you give me gifts, IF you become a good provider, IF you get a good report card at school." "If," is a conditional love, based upon future expectations. If these conditions are not met, then like a legal contract, love is broken. This is a selfish love because it is solely based upon future expectations. It is love that must be earned. Most marriages fail because they are based on this conditional love. Children are often heard saying, "I will be your best friend, IF you let me play with your new toy, till then I hate you." So the IF kind of love is a fickle, unstable, love. This is the childish love we are all born with. It is a worldly love of natural instincts. We need to mature out of the IF kind of love. A real man will.

- The "because of" love says, "I will love you BE-CAUSE you are now young and beautiful, BECAUSE I now desire you, BECAUSE you are now popular, BECAUSE you are now in good health or wealthy, BECAUSE I feel good when I am with you." This kind of love is common among teenagers because it is solely based upon the others current status. When someone proclaims, "I have fallen out of love," they have fallen out of the "because of" kind of love, not true love. This kind of love is not in tune with reality when it demands that things stay the same in an ever changing world. Like the IF kind of love, it is unstable and unpredictable. It is full of doubts and fears for what tomorrow might bring.

- True love is the, "In spite of love." It says, "I love you IN SPITE OF your faults, IN SPITE OF your being overweight and not beautiful, IN SPITE OF the times you are selfish and inconsiderate, IN SPITE OF when you sin against me." True love is unconditional. It is the love that God loves us with. It is a love we don't naturally possess, but must learn. It is an enduring love that doesn't keep a score card. It will always be there tomorrow, regardless of what we have done today. Romans 5:6-8 says, "For God demonstrates His own love toward us, in that while we were yet sinners, Christ died for us." Notice the contrast between conditional and unconditional love in this verse. Christ didn't die for us BECAUSE we were very good and worth dying for. Rather He died for us in SPITE OF the fact we were worthless sinners.

(Coach Daniel Bayless) "Love is like a house plant. When you first get it, it is beautiful. If you neglect it, it withers and eventually dies. If you feed it, water it, and devote time and attention to it, it will grow more beautiful than before."

"Love doesn't strut, doesn't have a swelled head, doesn't force itself on others, isn't always 'me first,' doesn't fly off the handle, doesn't keep score of the sins of others, doesn't revel when others grovel, takes pleasure in the flowering of truth, puts up with anything, trusts God always looks for the best, never looks back, but keeps going to the end. Love never dies..."

Every year I buy big beautiful hanging baskets of flowers for my front porch. I get them because they are so pretty and colorful, and I admire them and want them. The thing is; I stink at taking care of plants. Once I get them, and hang them up, I enjoy looking at them for a minute or when I happen to drive by the front of my house. Other than that, I tend to eventually forget about them, which means, I forget to water them. Then one day, I will venture out onto my front porch and notice the bright lovely flowers are droopy and the strong vibrant green stems are weak and browning. Frantically, I'll drown them in water trying to revive them, but, then once again, I forget about them. By the end of summer I always end up with hanging baskets of dead plants. What could have been beautiful and pleasing flowers eventually died because I didn't take the time to care for them and tend to them.

The people you love should feel completely safe and secure in your love. When someone is loved and they know it they radiate it from the inside out.

Love = trust. If someone trusts you with their heart, then don't betray that trust. Guard it. This is a deep and powerful love. There are people who go their entire lives without having someone love them on a deep and trusting level. If you have people in your life that offer that kind of love, don't take it lightly. When someone loves you like that, you now hold the power to hurt them deeply. Keep in mind, though, that you will be the one that truly misses out. You can't neglect someone who loves you to the point that their love is about to die and then try to drown them in love and not expect damage.

(Barry Farr) "Love really is what keeps life good. God tells us to put on many things, and become like Him in every way, but ultimately He tells us to put on love. Colossians 3:12-14 says, "So, chosen by God for this now life of love, dress in the wardrobe God picked out for you: compassion, kindness, humility, quiet strength, discipline. Be even-tempered, content with second place, quick to forgive an offense. Forgive as quickly and completely as the Master forgave you. And regardless of what else you put on, wear love. It's your basic, all-purpose garment. Never be without it." He clarifies that this is the same as putting Him on because God is Love. Why does he tell us to put on love? Because love makes sense of everything, makes everything work and allows us to enjoy the things we enjoy. Love is what makes the difference but love is not the gushy, sappy stuff that the movies and our culture try to make us believe. No, love is being willing to give your life, choose what another person wants over what you want and ultimately do what is best for the other person even if it costs you dearly."

"Inspired speech will be over some day; praying in tongues will end; understanding will reach its limit. We know only a portion of the truth, and what we say about God is always incomplete. But when the Complete arrives, our incompletes will be canceled. When I was an infant at by mother's breast, I gurgled and cooed like any infant. When I grew up, I left those infant ways for good. We don't yet see things clearly. We're squinting in a fog, peering through a mist. But it won't be long before the weather clears and the sun shines bright! We'll see it all then, see it all as clearly as God sees us, knowing him directly just as he knows us! But for right now, until that completeness, we have three things to do to lead us toward that consummation: Trust steadily in God, hope unswervingly, love extravagantly. And the best of the three is love" (1 Corinthians 13). ♥

Real men know how to love others.

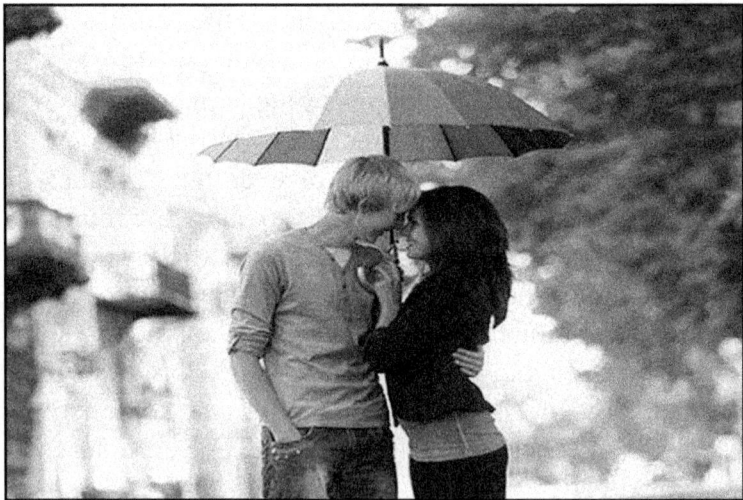

Chapter 9

DATING

"Guard your heart above all else, for it determines the course of your life" (Proverbs 4:23).

Guard your heart. When you guard something it means you are protecting it from harm in any form. Usually something you guard has great value. This verse tells us to guard our hearts because our hearts hold everything important in our life in them.

This may seem like a funny verse to start with on dating, but let me explain. Every time you casually date a girl you give a little piece of your heart to her. That piece, no matter how much you would like to take it back you can't. It's gone. That's one less piece of your heart you have to give to your future wife. Your future wife deserves your entire heart saved just for her.

(Coach Daniel Bayless) "Dating someone you know deep down you won't spend your life with could be a lot of fun, but it will lead to a lot of pain."

Dating someone to meet our own needs is unhealthy. We all want intimacy with another person and want to have someone we can trust in, but often we don't have patience. When this happens, we end up dating someone just for the sake of dating them. No true passion is involved. No future is possible. But our "needs" are temporarily being met. This is not honoring to ourselves or the person we're dating, and most importantly it's not honoring to God.

Intimacy is about getting to know another person at a deeper level and allowing them to know who you are.

> "So flee youthful passions and pursue righteousness, faith, love, and peace, along with those who call on the Lord from a pure heart" (2 Timothy 2:22).

You may think it's too late for you to have a pure heart. It's not! God's love purifies everything! Just pray and ask Him to make your heart new and put your trust in Him. Then live your life for him. The above verse says flee from youthful passions. When you flee you don't just casually walk away. No, you run! You do whatever it takes to get away. If you know you struggle in an area of temptation don't set yourself up to fail! If you can't handle dating girls without having to have sex with her then don't date. Don't put yourself in that temptation. If you can't handle dating a girl without having to play with her heart, in order to make you feel better about yourself, then don't date. If you can't date a girl without falling head over heels in love with her without really knowing her then don't date. Wait until God and you have worked on the areas you struggle with. Until then, get to know girls in group settings and set your boundaries.

(Marca Deimund) "Be the person you want to

be with because you attract what you are. It is never too late to let God begin to do a great work in you! Do not date a non-Christian. Period! If your friends don't think this girl is good for you, LISTEN! Your friends usually tell you what you want to hear, so if they don't like her, run the other way! Love is never enough; respect and love are great companions. Do you respect or can she respect the way you/she treats her parents; teachers; boss or any others in authority over you? In other words do your actions or hers embarrass you/her in anyway? You/she will eventually treat each other the same way. A mother of one of my school kids told her son, 'Don't touch her anywhere you wouldn't touch me' I love this! Group date until you are older. Date a girl one year/ grade older or younger than you; too much of an age difference until you are 18 or 19 can lead to heartache!"

Before you even consider dating you should have an idea about the type of girl you want to be with. Now, some guys, right off the bat will say "she's gotta be hot!" well, keep in mind, something hot usually burns you. Instead of putting a lot of focus on outer beauty, make a list of at least ten character traits a woman MUST have in order for you to consider dating her and ten character traits she must NOT have. At the top of your list of musts should be that she should be a Christian.

It may sound a bit like a job interview but usually the purpose of dating is to find a wife. This is the person you are making a commitment to God and everyone else that you will spend the rest of your life with. The.Rest. Of.Your.Life, that can be a very long time. This is the woman who will be the future mother to your children. Do not rush this. Really find out who this person is that you are giving so much time and attention to. Is she honest with her parents, family, friends and boss? If not, then why do you think she will be honest with you? Are there little things that get under your skin when you're around her? Those little things can turn into huge annoyances over time. Until you really get to know her don't spend a lot of alone time together. See how she interacts with others. Most importantly, keep the "love" word out of your mouth until you are truly 100% ready to commit. Girls take this word to heart very quickly and very strongly. Don't just tell her that because you know it's what she wants to hear. Explain to her you would rather save that word for your one true love. Don't play with her emotions. Girls are very emotional beings and can easily get hurt. Do you really want some guy playing your daughter that way some day?

> (Kwasi Ofori-Yeboah) "Set boundaries when you start dating someone, so that both of you know what the boundaries are. This will help prevent misunderstanding and confusion as to your intentions and plans. Some relationships falter because of honest misunderstandings and miscommunications. You want to guard against that, hence the importance of boundaries and clarity of expectations."

I hear guys say all the time, "We're just guys, we can't help it," or "she wanted it too." Alright, well, here's what I think. My dog Jenna can control herself whenever she needs to go to the bathroom and she waits until someone is home to let her outside. She knows where the door is and has trained herself to go to the door whenever she needs to go out. Jenna is a dog, an animal. She can control herself fairly well. Guys are far above being just a simple minded animal. You are more than your lusts. I love chocolate. You can even say it is my weakness. But I honestly can say I can be surrounded by chocolate and know how to walk away without HAVING to have it.

As far as the "she wanted it too" goes, be the stronger person. Set your boundaries ahead of time and let her know what you are looking for in a relationship and what you will and will not do. Be a man of integrity and honor this young lady by showing her she is safe with you. Protect her purity for her future husband. Until you have both said "I do" then what she has to offer you does not belong to you. It is intended for someone else. Would you want some guy or worse yet, many guys stealing something priceless and special that was only meant for you? Whenever you have sex with a girl you degrade her and yourself. A real man knows how to control himself. A boy knows how to take what he wants and not think of the consequences or of others it might affect. There's no need for you to lower your standards and have sex with a girl in order to have some feel good attention for a little while. That's not going to get you a good woman for life. Honestly, a good woman doesn't want what everyone else has already had. She wants someone who has saved themselves, heart and body just for her.

(Stephanie Schraeder) "Remember that she is someone's daughter and treat her with the respect that you would expect your daughter one day to be treated with. She is also someone's princess and should be treated like one, even when she doesn't deserve it."

It's true...someday you just very well could have a daughter of your own. How do you want her thought of by a boy? How do you want her treated? What kind of standards do you want her to have? Then set the example now so you won't be a hypocrite in the future. Nobody likes to hear stories from their parents as they explain all the mistakes they made and wished they didn't. Be that man of good character now, and help the women you are dating to not have regrets.

> (Coach Lance Roweton) "I know we all know guys that treat girls with disrespect. Don't be that guy. If you go on a date treat her with respect. Make her feel safe. Have fun and be relaxed. Most importantly be yourself. Don't take yourself too seriously and don't be afraid to laugh at yourself. At the end of the night decide whether or not you want to go out with her again and move on from there."

Being you is so important. If you're not being the real you then you are really cheating yourself out of a genuine relationship. If you don't like something then say so. If you do like something then say so. Simply don't be a fake. By being a fake you will not discover if the two of you truly are compatible. I'm going to tell a bit of a story that's been around awhile, but I'm going to put a different twist on it. You see, this story was meant to show you how compromising your standards just a little bit are not good.

I read a story online once that illustrated this very well:

> *Some years ago when I was a pastor, I walked into my church office after a Sunday morning service to find a sandwich bag on my desk containing three chocolate brownies. Some thoughtful and anonymous saint, who knew my love for chocolate, had placed them there, along with a piece of paper that had a short story written on it. I immediately sat down and began eating the first brownie as I read the following story:*

Two teenagers asked their father if they could go to the theater to watch a movie that all their friends had seen. After reading some reviews about the movie on the internet, he denied their request.

"Aw dad, why not?" they complained. "It's rated PG-13, and we're both older than thirteen!"

Dad replied; "Because that movie contains nudity and portrays immorality, which is something that God hates, as being normal and acceptable behavior."

"But dad, those are just very small parts of the movie! That's what our friends who've seen it have told us. The movie is two hours long and those scenes are just a few minutes of the total time! It's based on a true story and good triumphs over evil, and there are other redeeming themes like courage and self-sacrifice. Even the Christian move review websites say that!"

"My answer is 'no,' and that is my final answer. You are welcome to stay home tonight, invite some of your friends over, and watch one of the good videos we have in our home collection. But you will not go and watch that film. End of discussion."

The two teenagers walked dejectedly into the family room and slumped down on the couch. As they sulked, they were surprised to hear the sounds of their father preparing something in the kitchen. They soon recognized the wonderful aroma of brownies baking in the oven, and one of the teenagers said to the other, "Dad must be feeling guilty, and now he's going to try to make it up to us with some fresh brownies. Maybe we can soften him with lots of praise when he brings them out to us and persuade him to let us go to that movie after all."

About that time I began eating the second brownie from the sandwich bag and wondered if there was some connection to the brownies I was eating and the brownies in the story. I kept reading...

The teens were not disappointed. Soon their father appeared with a plate of warm brownies which he offered to his kids. They each took one. Their father said,

"Before you eat, I want to tell you something: I love you both so much."

The teenagers smiled at each other with knowing glances. Dad was softening.

"That is why I've made these brownies with the very best ingredients. I've made them from scratch. Most of the ingredients are even organic. The best organic flour. The best free-range eggs. The best organic sugar. Premium vanilla and chocolate."

The brownies looked mouth-watering, and the teens began to become a little impatient with their dad's long speech.

"But I want to be perfectly honest with you. There is one ingredient I added that is not usually found in brownies. I got that ingredient from our own back yard. But you needn't worry, because I only added the tiniest bit of that ingredient to your brownies. The amount of the portion is practically insignificant. So go ahead, take a bite and let me know what you think."

"Dad, would you mind telling us what that mystery ingredient is before we eat?"

"Why? The portion I added was so small. Just a teaspoonful. You won't even taste it."

"Come on, dad; just tell us what that ingredient is."

"Don't worry! It is organic, just like the other ingredients."

"Dad!"

"Well, OK, if you insist. That secret ingredient is organic...dog poop."

I immediately stopped chewing that second brownie and I spit it out into the waste basket by my desk. I continued reading, now fearful of the paragraphs that still remained.

Both teens instantly dropped their brownies back on the plate and began inspecting their fingers with horror.

"DAD! Why did you do that? You've tortured us by making us smell those brownies cooking for the last half hour, and now you tell us that you added dog poop! We can't eat these brownies!" "Why not? The amount of dog poop is very small compared to the rest of the ingredients. It won't hurt you. It's been cooked right along with the other ingredients. You won't even taste it. It has the same consistency as the brownies. Go ahead and eat!" "No, Dad...NEVER!"

"And that is the same reason I won't allow you to go watch that movie. You won't tolerate a little dog poop in your brownies, so why should you tolerate a little immorality in your movies? We pray that God will not lead us unto temptation, so how can we in good conscience entertain ourselves with something that will imprint a sinful image in our minds that will lead us into temptation long after we first see it?

> *I discarded what remained of the second brownie as well as the entire untouched third brownie. What had been irresistible a minute ago had become detestable. And only because of the very slim chance that what I was eating was slightly polluted. (Surely it wasn't...but I couldn't convince myself.)*
>
> *What a good lesson about purity! Why do we tolerate any sin? "Hate evil, you who love the Lord (Ps 97:10).*

So...The actual point of this story is obvious, but there is also another point that might not be so obvious. If that pan of brownies were just sitting on the counter, they would look good and smell good and taste good. But they weren't really brownies like we desire them to be. They were gussied up dog poop. Now, I'm not saying when we aren't being ourselves we are like dog poop! I'm saying when we don't let others see the real us, we are deceiving them into believing we are something we're not. Just like the dad in this story somewhat deceived his kids. In the end, the kids were really disappointed and probably a little resentful to be honest.

If you want a relationship that will last, and then be honest with whom you are. If she doesn't like you for who you are then she is not the one meant for you. Save your heart for the one it's meant for.

> (Coach Clayton McCullah) "Real men treat women as if they are a priceless treasure to be won and not an object to be thrown away once they are through with them. Women are special creatures and a real man will treat them such."

Don't, under any circumstance; play with a woman's heart. Don't tell her things you know she wants to hear just to make yourself feel good or for your personal gain. Real men don't do that. This applies to any woman whether you are dating her or just friends. Protect the women in your life from physical and emotional harm. Their hearts are beautiful things that can get crushed easily.

I recently watched the movie *Oz the Great and Powerful*, and it demonstrated this perfectly. Oz was a flirt, and any women that came within his sight he made them feel extremely special. He made them feel like they meant something personal to him. He even gave them a special music box (the exact same one to every woman) saying it was his grandmother's. Oh how he played with their hearts. When one of the women's fathers found out, he (being a real and protective man) chased Oz into an air balloon where he floated until he ended up in a tornado which carried him to a strange land. The first person he encountered was a beautiful woman with an innocent sweet heart. He instantly started playing his game with her by making her feel special to him. He even gave her a music box. By the time she led him to the castle where she lived with her sister she was head over heels in love and talking marriage (in which he never once discouraged even though it was obvious he did not really want that). Her eyes soon became open when she caught him telling the same lies to her sister and flirting with her. It crushed her heart and destroyed her trust. She was so hurt she chose to have a spell turned on her that would cause her not to have love in her heart anymore. Because of this her outer appearance reflected her inner and she turned into a hideous wicked witch.

The moral of this story...When a man acts like a selfish little boy and plays with an innocent trusting heart it can turn a beautiful woman into an ugly witch. And maybe, just maybe some foolish guy is playing your future wife's heart. Don't let it happen. Stand up and do what's right. Be a real man.

(Paul Dillman) "Finding a good woman as a partner for life sometimes takes years. It took me 34 years to find Beth and where I'm lacking, such as how to talk to people and showing love, she has helped me. So when you meet and date women, take your time getting to really know them and understand them. Let God guide you to make the right choice. You will feel the chemistry between the both of you when it happens."

Sometimes, people spend more time shopping for a car or choosing a career than they do choosing their spouse. Don't just fall for every girl that smiles at you and makes your ego swell. As hard as it is to believe, there are girl players out there. They jump from guy to guy quickly getting bored. Girls know just what to do and just what to say to capture a guy's attention. Ever have a girl tell you she dreamed about you? Yeeeaaah, that's always a favorite line. Or how about how they are scared of something and you make them feel safe? Guys are natural protectors, and girls know this. Ask around about a girl you're interested in and see what others might say about her character then use your own good judgment and take things slow. Believe me, girls do this. They talk, and they ask their friends opinions. You have the rest of your life. Don't rush this.

(Papa & Granny) "When you start dating, always show respect to your date. Remember, she has feelings that can be hurt. Talk things over. You are not the only one who has to have his way. Don't be ashamed to say I'm sorry when you are wrong.

Just have fun doing things together. It is not about sex. That is something between a man and woman who are married."

When you are dating someone, more than likely you will have some arguments. This is a good thing. If not, one of you is not being honest about your feelings. That's called conflict avoidance and it's not healthy in any relationship. Learn how to talk things out, not yell things out. Be mature and take into consideration what she is trying to say. Be respectful toward her even in your disagreements. If one of you is always getting their way this is a sign of a serious problem also. Sometimes the hardest thing to do is say I'm sorry. Usually the stronger person will be the first to utter those words. A lot of times that is all someone is looking for; just a sincere apology. Talk your problems out; compromise with each other. If you can't figure out how to do this while you're dating it can lead to disaster.

(Barry Farr) "I would encourage you not to date unless you intend to find a wife. A great deal of pain comes from persons dating just for the sport or because they are following the crowd."

Don't chase love. Let it find you. The term, falling in love, is so misleading. Usually when a person falls, they get hurt. Depending on the distance they fall, the more they end up getting hurt. The same goes for love. If you just fall in love, more than likely you will end up getting hurt or hurting someone. Instead, grow in love. Whenever you grow something it takes time. You nurture it, and slowly, after a while, something beautiful develops. Take your time getting to know each other as friends without any romantic involvement. Learn about each other and find out if you are really compatible. Whenever "love" gets thrown into the relationship it sometimes blinds a person's judgment. Learn to like each other first. Become friends and friends only. Over time, you will go through fun times and hard times. You will see each other happy, sad, angry, stressed, lazy, sick, hurting, excited, afraid and any other emotion you could possibly go through. You will see how this girl handles herself during these times, and she will see how you handle yourself. You will either decide, "Whoa! I don't think this is what I had in mind! This person is totally nuts!" Or, you will become best friends. As best friends you will learn to care for each other and be there for each other. You will learn to put each other before you own self. Again, save the mushy romance. Believe me, it's worth waiting for! You might be thinking, this really is taking a long time! There's an old saying, "Good things come to those who wait." It's true. As you're getting to know each other, you will be busy with the rest of your life, such as school and work.

Before you know it, if your friendship has grown closer and deepened, you will find yourself growing more and more in love. It will be a strong love based on mutual trust and respect. That mutual trust and respect is well worth taking your time and effort for.

There are all kinds of young women out there just looking for a ring, and a prince to put it on her finger, and live then to happily ever after. Unfortunately it is usually in that order. Be smart when it comes to dating. My advice to help save a lot of emotional pain...Court, instead of date, and hopefully it will keep you out of court in the future! Courtship is about honestly exploring each other's lives without the romantic interaction, until after a commitment has been made to marry. When you court someone you are basically seeing if you can become best friends, and discovering if this individual is someone you can commit to marrying.

Chapter 10

COLLEGE

"Observe people who are good at their work-skilled workers are always in demand and admired; they don't take a backseat to anyone" (Proverbs 22:29).

(Gina Green) "Finish your degree, no matter what. If you don't, you'll always wish you had, no matter how successful you become."

You should have a life goal planned out. What do you want for your life? Where do you see yourself ten years from now? Most guys will say they see themselves in a good career and with a wife and kids owning a home and driving a nice car. Great plan! Now, start out slow and take the necessary steps to get there.

You didn't ride a bike before you learned how to walk.

Write out the steps you need to take to help you reach your goals. A good example would look something like this:

1. Go to college and get your degree

2. Find work and start building your career

3. Create a home for yourself

4. Be able to take care of yourself financially

5. Date with the purpose of finding a wife

6. Marry and move in together – notice I said marry first

7. Enjoy time together as a couple (This is very important. You won't have this time again for a long time after you have kids, and if you marry just to have kids, your marriage could be in trouble after the kids are grown and gone.)

8. Time to start a family

Getting your plan out of order can work, but it can also lead to a lot of struggles. Going back to school as an adult is difficult. You have so many other responsibilities to focus on and someone somewhere will feel short changed, and you will feel stressed out.

Get your degree. It's important. Take however long you must take. There will be plenty of time for all the other stuff. But, while you're young and single, get you degree.

(Papa & Granny) "As you look and find you a college, remember this is not a place for you to go and party. But a place for you to use your mind that God gave you and what you have learned in school. Just remember, this will help you the rest of your life in what you will be and how you will handle everything that comes your way."

Most kids, when they get out of high school, are so eager to be independent that they make foolish choices. They get in the mindset that they need to have the full college experience. They have heard others tell stories about all the crazy things they did in college, and they fall for the idea that they too must do all of this in order to enjoy college.

In reality, college is the first time in your life where you will be totally responsible for yourself. It is also a time where you are paying for an education that will shape your entire future plans. Why would you take this lightly for a few good times? Most colleges plan all kinds of activities for the students to take part in and I encourage you to do so! But your studies and classes should ALWAYS come first. If something or someone is distracting you from this then it's time to refocus and remove the distraction. This is how you succeed. This is where you need to grow up and be a man. College is a place you pay to get a good education in order to have a successful future. That's it. People who are not as focused have turned it into a party time all the time. Don't fall for this trap.

(Paul Dillman) "God has implanted in you, talents and gifts. It's up to you to use and do something with these talents and gifts. If you don't they will be no good."

God has given everyone talents and gifts of some kind. Most of us have a pretty good idea of what we are good at. You and only you are responsible for growing these talents and gifts into something amazing. You can't blame your past or the people in it for holding you back. No excuses. If you want to succeed then take on a successful attitude and go after what you want. Study hard. Attend all classes. Get help when you don't understand something. Ask questions.

(Coach Lance Roweton) "In the next ten years you will make several life changing decisions. The first decision you will make is where to go to college. You will have several colleges to choose from when it comes time. Go to the school that best suits you. Do they have the degree that you want to major in? What does it cost? Think about location. Do you feel comfortable being really far from home? Do you like the idea of staying close to 'home' and living at home? Do you want to go far enough from home that you can be your own person but still close enough that if you needed help from home 'someone' could help you? Consider all these factors and more and then like I said, go to the school that best suits you."

It's a privilege to attend college. If you find a college you want to attend then make it happen. There are all kinds of ways to pay for college. Not having the money is no excuse. You can get a job or jobs. Apply for scholarships and student loans. Look into a work study program. Basically, if you really want to go you will find a way.

(Kwasi Ofori-Yeboah) "College is very important and I cannot encourage you enough to do all you can to go to college. The piece of paper you receive after college will open a lot of doors. College is worth the time, effort and resources you will have to expend because in the long run, the benefits will far outweigh whatever sacrifices you endured to get that degree. College will ask a lot of you, time management, planning, self-discipline, and determination. But all these traits will serve you well in life, long after your college days are over. You will also form life-long friendships in college. As well, the knowledge and skills you acquire in college will shape and transform your life for the better."

You're going to learn more at college than what is taught in the books. These lessons will help you the rest of your life.

In high school, if you didn't get to school on time you received a tardy. If you missed a class you received an unexcused absence. More than likely the teachers were not happy with you and would say something about it. If you didn't turn in an assignment the teacher might remind you and you would receive points off your grade. Basically, you were always held accountable by someone; your parents or teachers usually.

In college you are totally responsible for yourself. If you're late you are counted absent and receive a zero that day. The instructor doesn't care what your excuse is. If you don't do your assignments you receive a zero. Most instructors do not accept late work at all. It's your responsibility to do your work on time. The instructor doesn't care what your excuse is. They get paid (by you through your pricey tuition) to teach, not to listen to lame excuses. Therefore, manage your time well, have self-discipline, prioritize and stay focused. Again, your success is up to you and no one else.

(Griff Schoen) "College is expensive. If at all possible, find a way to pay for it without loans. If that means a summer job, then so be it. Also, there are thousands of grants and scholarships. I once heard of a woman who sat down with her son the summer after he graduated high school. All they did every day was applying for grants and scholarships. He ended up with all 4 years of college paid for with no loans. Trust me; you don't want to owe $40,000 after you graduate."

Depending on how much time and effort you want to

put into it there all kinds of scholarships every year that go unclaimed. It is work, and most of the time a lot of writing, but well worth it. Don't pass up the little scholarships. Those little scholarships combined can add up! Nothing worth having in life comes easy. If things are constantly just being handed to you then that means you are more than likely taking advantage of someone else's generosity and kindness. Life shouldn't be about handouts. When you work hard for something, you appreciate it much more. Do the work necessary to pay for your college and you will be proud of your degree!

If scholarships are not enough to pay for your tuition then don't be afraid to take out a student loan. Sometimes having that loan helps keep you focused. Knowing you yourself will have to pay that money back will make you want to not waste it by blowing off assignments and classes.

If you do take out student loans only take out the amount you really need. Keep in mind too that this is a good debt. Getting a top education and a degree is priceless.

(Marca Deimund) "When you start college don't be surprised if you change your major; you are learning who you are and be true to your heart! You may even change colleges; it is OK! Just finish the semester."

It's an age old question asked by everyone, "What do I want to be when I grow up?" Everyone thinks they need to know the answer to that before they even get out of high school. My daughter Bailey, when she was five, announced she wanted to be a roller skating, cheer-leading, cowgirl when she grew up. Since then she has changed her mind multiple times (thank goodness). You can't be expected to know what you want to do for the rest of your life when you haven't even gotten out on your own and found out who you really are and what you like and don't like.

There are all kinds of people at college who can guide you with this decision. It's a big world out there and the careers are endless! If you find you really don't enjoy what you're majoring in then talk to your adviser and look into something different! No one says you HAVE to stick with what you started out with. Don't settle for your first choice in majors just because you want to get out of school faster and get on with life. You will have PLENTY of time for life. Soak up what you can in the moment you're living in and don't rush it, or short-change yourself, because you are in a hurry to get to the next step in your life. Take your time and do it right.

(Claudia Pyle) "Pyle Family rules for college...1. No Drugs 2. No Credit Cards 3. No Cults"

While going away to college can be an exciting time it's also a time you will be exposed to things you might not have ever encountered before, and pressured into participating in them hard core.

The party scene in college can look huge! It can range from just a few people getting together in a dorm to an out and out full blown wild and crazy party where anything goes.

According to www.Dailyinfographic.com, "The only illicit drug that has lost popularity instead of gaining popularity in the last 20 years was acid...Alcohol has also declined, but from 88% to 80% it is still safe to say the majority of college students love their booze.

The new drug of choice for college students is a performance enhancing drug called Adderall, Ritalin and many others. Over 50% of students have tried these drugs without a prescription. This 'medicine' is over-prescribed to our nation's youth and is way too available on college campuses. The side-effects of mixing a college student's two favorite drugs: speed and alcohol can be devastating. The energy provided by certain amphetamines can keep people awake and drinking until they poison themselves."

The average college student parties 10+ hours a week compared to 7.25 hours spent studying.

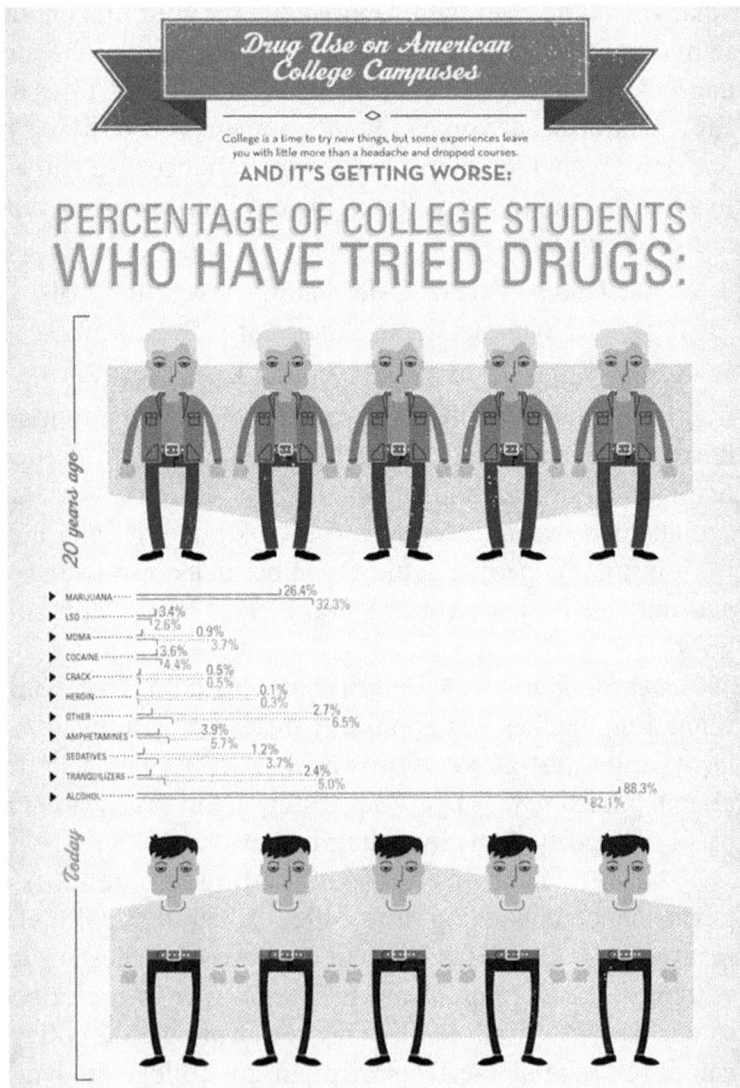

Drug Use on American College Campuses

College is a time to try new things, but some experiences leave you with little more than a headache and dropped courses.
AND IT'S GETTING WORSE:

PERCENTAGE OF COLLEGE STUDENTS WHO HAVE TRIED DRUGS:

20 years ago

- MARIJUANA — 26.4% / 32.3%
- LSD — 13.4% / 2.6%
- MDMA — 0.9% / 3.7%
- COCAINE — 3.6% / 4.4%
- CRACK — 0.5% / 0.5%
- HEROIN — 0.1% / 0.3%
- OTHER — 2.7% / 6.5%
- AMPHETAMINES — 3.9% / 5.7%
- SEDATIVES — 1.2% / 3.7%
- TRANQUILIZERS — 2.4% / 5.0%
- ALCOHOL — 88.3% / 82.1%

Today

The college student's drug of choice? Booze. Male students average 82 drinks a month and females average 59 drinks a month. Out of college students 82% drink and 50% admit to having blacked out at least once.

So you might say, "Well, that's all interesting but I don't drink or do drugs. How does this affect me?"

You will have a dorm mate. Your dorm mate will have friends. Choose your dorm mate carefully....

1. 3.36 Million Students get behind the wheel drunk each year

2. 696,000 People are assaulted by intoxicated students each year

3. 599,000 Students suffer alcohol-related injuries each year

4. 97,000 People are sexually assaulted by intoxicated students

5. 1,825 Students die from alcohol poisoning each year

6. 31% of Students meet the criteria for a clinical diagnosis of alcohol abuse each year

7. 25% of Students face academic consequences as a result of alcohol abuse each year

8. 11% of Students damage private property while intoxicated each year

9. 90% of Campus rapes are fueled by drugs and alcohol

10. 31% of Students have missed a class due to drug or alcohol abuse

11. 22% of Students have failed an exam due to drug or alcohol abuse

12. 159,000: Number of freshmen who will drop out each year because of drug or alcohol abuse.

The point is, this is a major problem on college campuses. Even if you don't participate, it will still be around

you. This is where your integrity and morals will be tested. This is where your friendship abilities will be tested.
Choose friends who have the same drive to succeed as you
and whose standards are as high as yours.

Credit Cards

As far as credit cards go just don't get one. The credit
card companies target college students and flood them with
easy access to fast money. Those little credit card purchases add up VERY quickly and then the bill arrives and your
left standing with your mouth open wondering how you're
going to pay it off. Every month you don't pay it off they
add interest so you're actually paying even more for something.

As soon as you get a credit card application just tear
it up and throw it away. Save yourself a lot of stress! My
grandfather always said, "If you can't pay cash you just
don't need it."

Cults

Cults—well, there are a lot of interesting ideas out
there. You have GOT to be strong in your faith in God and
know what you believe. Your faith will be put to the test in
college among your peers and professors. They will belittle
you and make you feel like the dumbest person on earth for
believing in God. But...the Bible says in Philippians 2:8-
11, "He humbled himself in obedience to God and died a
criminal's death on a cross. Therefore, God elevated him to
the place of highest honor and gave him the name above all
other names, that at the name of Jesus every knee should
bow in heaven and on earth and under the earth, and every
tongue confess that Jesus Christ is Lord, to the glory of
God the Father."

There will come a day when all these people who might
mock you for your beliefs will bow down and confess that

Jesus is Lord.

The Bible also warns us in Matthew 10:32-33, "Everyone who acknowledges me before others, I will also acknowledge before my Father in heaven. But whoever denies me before others, I will disown before my Father in heaven."

A real man stands up for what he believes in and does not cower from those who try to persuade him against it. Find a church and get involved in their college group. All college towns have churches that will have college programs. This would be one college activity that would be worth your time! And if you're looking for a good Christian woman to someday marry this would probably be a better place to meet her than at a drunken party! Again, keep your goals in mind and set your priorities. Make attending church a big one.

(Coach Daniel Bayless) "College has very little to do with intelligence. Drive + Hard work = success in college."

There are going to be classes that are just going to take you to your limit. You're not going to enjoy them and you will make excuses why you're not doing well in them. Don't. Just do the work that needs to be done. Get help when needed. You are paying for that help! There are labs and tutoring available. Use it! You're only going to do as well as you try.

Anyone who knows me knows I hate math with a passion. I don't understand it and I get easily frustrated with it. I actually have a fear of math! I've let this fear keep me from getting my degree. So at the age of 44 I decided to go back to school. The first class I had to take was a math class. I gave myself pep talks and got all my stuff ready and took myself to school. As I was walking up the sidewalk on a beautiful sunny day I was enjoying the birds singing and all the other college students strolling around. I thought to myself, "Hey, I can do this. It's not that big of a deal." I then walked into the building, straight past the doors of my classroom and went promptly into the bathroom and threw up everything that could have possibly been in me! Yep, that's exactly how much I feared and hated math. I was the oldest in a class full of college football players. I worked, had children, a husband, my elderly parents, and a home to take care of. I would go to class and listen to the "boys" complain and use excuses on why they didn't have their homework done or why they failed a test because they didn't have time to study. It annoyed me. Every day I spent hours studying and doing homework. I asked for help from everyone I could think could help me. I took notes on everything in front of me. I drove the son of my heart, Jake crazy, as he was the one who patiently explained to me how letters and numbers could both be a part of math. In the end I passed. Nope, I didn't just pass. I got an A! When I handed my final exam in, my professor handed me an envelope. I got to my car and opened it. Inside was a card. What she wrote on it touched my heart and made me realize my positive attitude, drive, and hard work did not go unnoticed. "You are an amazing woman!! I admire you so much and want you to know I enjoyed having you in this class so much—a true blessing! I pray you are successful and make it through college more easily than this has been. Keep in touch!"

Just do the work. A real man doesn't complain. He just does what needs to be done.

> (Barry Farr) "I do not have a lot to say about college except that I think you should give it a try. I enjoyed college so much that I spent 7 years in college."

Chapter 11

CHOOSING A CAREER

"I will instruct you and teach you in the way you should go; I will counsel you with my eye upon you" (Psalm 32:8 ESV).

(Coach Daniel Bayless) "Go with what you enjoy. Money is important, but MUCH less important than loving your job. Also, look at where there are opportunities. In my case, I knew teaching would not pay a lot, but I also knew I would love it. I actually enjoy history more than English but history teachers that coach are a dime a dozen while an English teacher that coaches three sports is very hard to find. Coaching is actually my love so I went with English because it is so much more marketable. I also received two post graduate degrees so that I could make enough money to support my family doing what I love."

This is where your college degree will pay off! You have worked hard to earn it, now use it! You will spend a large portion of your day at your job. Find something that will make you happy. Money is important, but if you are miserable day in and day out for a large portion of your day then you are going to be one unhappy man.

(Griff Schoen) "Mark Twain once said, 'If you are doing something that you love, you'll never work a day in your life.' Jobs are fine for paying the bills but when it comes to a career, make it something you enjoy. Don't become a lawyer, for instance, simply because someone told you it pays well. Money isn't everything and certainly won't buy happiness. If you love it, you will find a way to make money at it..."

When interviewing for a job, make sure you look your best! From the top of your head to the bottom of your shoes you should be put together. First impressions are VERY important! Getting a second chance at a first impression is difficult, if not impossible. Words account for about 7 percent of your initial first impression, your vocal quality about 38 percent and 55 percent is based on appearance.

Also, know your manners and etiquette! It can make a major difference. The more you learn and know about etiquette the more it is going to enhance your professional career and image. I heard a true story once of three college grads who were all applying for the same job in a major corporation. The position was high pay with excellent benefits; a perfect stepping stone on the right career path. All three applicants had outstanding qualities and their interviews went perfect. The CEO of the company invited them all out to supper that night at a nice restaurant. At the end of the meal he had made his decision. All of the candidates were well qualified for the position, but his final choice was made on the one who had the best manners and etiquette. That was who he wanted representing his company.

There are many people out there looking for work.

What are you going to do to stand out among them?

(Kwasi Ofori-Yeboah) "Sometimes we don't know what we want to do when we grow up, other times we do. Whatever the case might be in your situation, there are a few important factors to consider in career choice decisions. We all have our proclivities and are drawn to certain goals and careers in life. That should be one of the guiding principles when you are deciding what to do in life. Is there a career that is appealing to you that you find yourself doing in the future? If so, what will it take to enter that career? Obviously answers to these questions will influence your college choice and course options. Even if you are not sure what you want to be when you grow up, resolve to go to college. Because while there, you are likely to find certain fields of study to be more suitable to your strengths and that might point you in the direction of your future career. As far as career goes, you want to do something that you enjoy doing. You don't want a job where it is a chore and pain to think about, let alone go there. Unfortunately, without a college degree, you might wind up doing jobs that you don't really enjoy. So there is a strong connection between college education and viable career choices, that is why, once again, I will strongly encourage you to pursue a college degree. It will enrich your life personally and open career opportunities. You will want to enjoy what you do for a living, and college will help in the regard."

Make sure when you go for an interview you are prepared also to ask questions. Find out as much as you can about the business. Make sure you are not just selling yourself well, but that you are compatible with the place you will be working.

Also, don't hesitate to ask what type of package they will offer you. It's not just about a pay check. Ask about retirement plans and if they contribute toward them. Ask about health insurance. Does it include dental and vision? Ask if there is a continuing education allowance so you can keep up on all the latest. Ask about vacation time and sick leave.

(Coach Lance Roweton) "In the next 10 years you will choose a career. My advice to you on this is to choose something you like to do and make sure what you like to do can support your wife and kids. In my opinion, this is the key to a happy marriage; that a man takes care of his wife and kids financially. Once you get into your career do everything you can to better yourself in that career. If there are more classes you can take to better your pay then you take those classes. If you can work longer hours to advance yourself in your career then you do it early on and get a jump on things. Be ambitious in your career. Figure out how things work at every level and see if you can be a boss someday rather than an employee. Be loyal to your boss. Be honest with your boss. Work hard."

"Anyone who does not provide for their relatives, and especially for their own household, has denied the faith and is worse than an unbeliever" (1 Timothy 5:8).

Get a job. Provide for yourself and your family. Do not rely on others to pay your way through life. This includes the government. If you can't take care of yourself you sure can't take care of a family, so don't start one (including getting married) until you can. It's not fair to them and it's not fair to everyone who does work to have to support those who are too lazy to get out and find work. If you can't find work then create work until you can. Go door to door if you have to. Work a job flipping burgers if you have to. But work. There is no excuse not to. None!

(Paul Dillman) "Focus on what you really want to be, and something you really enjoy, and know God has given you a gift at doing. Then you won't get burned out at it and jump from career to career."

No job is perfect. There will be things you just don't like about your work. I believe 90% of our happiness comes from our attitude. Don't grumble while working. If you have a career, consider it a blessing, especially when you have a wife and kids. This is your way of showing you love and care about them...by providing for them. So if you are always unhappy and complaining and finding fault with your job you just might be saying to your family you think they are a burden. Man up. Change your attitude and do what needs to be done. No one likes a constant complainer.

(Gina Green) "Do something you have a passion for. Don't go into a career just for the money. Money can't make you happy, but following a passion will. Teaching brings me joy every day, and I can't imagine doing anything else. Find a job you love like that."

Your career shouldn't be just about the money. Some men get so wrapped up in money that they forget the simple pleasures in life that are free. You don't need a big boat to enjoy the lake. God made it perfect just the way it is. You don't need an expensive car. Cars should be reliable.

They carry your most precious possessions when you have a family, and most of the time the more expensive cars are not the most reliable. You don't need a huge house. Families scatter, the bigger the house and forget how to spend quality time together. Basically, what I'm saying is, don't live for "things." Live to please God and take care of yourself and others. Enjoy life. Don't be tied to a career you hate just because it pays for pricey stuff.

> (Papa & Granny) "When you get a job remember a tenth of your money goes back to God. If you give Him his part you can make it on the ninety percent that is left. Then start your retirement fund so you will always have something to fall back on as you get older. (Papa) Find a job you enjoy doing. You will be spending the majority of your day there. If you are doing something you don't enjoy it will make you miserable and that will affect others in your life. Your job is something you should be proud of and like."

How you spend your first paycheck will set the course on how you plan to budget your money. Yes, budget your money or you will see it fly right out of your wallet! Pay God first, always. He blesses you with so much and only asks that you give 10 percent back to Him while you keep 90 percent for yourself.

After that you should start out saving 10 percent into a savings account. This should be untouchable.

Fidelity Investments put together an age-based saving guideline with a range of savings goals:

- At age 35, you should have saved an amount equal to your annual salary.

- At age 45, you should have saved three times your annual salary.

- At 55, you should have five times your salary.

- When you retire at age 67, you should have eight times your annual pay.

- Begin saving in a workplace retirement plan, such as a 401(k), at age 25. You save continuously and without interruption until age 67.

These are just one way of saving. Look into what is best for you. Starting out though, I would suggest taking your check and tithing (giving to God) 10%, then putting 10% in a savings account. Now you are ready to pay bills. This should ALWAYS take place before spending any money on anything else. Paying off debt should come before fun. A real man is responsible for his debt.

(Barry Farr) "When it comes to choosing a career just remember you may not end up where you originally planned but I would encourage you to not settle for whatever happens. Make sure you eventually enjoy the career you choose. I cannot think of many things more difficult than working at a job day in and day out that you hate."

Chapter 12

HARD WORK

"Whatever you do, work heartily, as for the Lord and not for men" (Colossians 3:23 ESV).

(Gina Green) " *'Nothing in the world is worth having or doing unless it means effort, pain, difficulty...I have never in my life envied a human being who had an easy life. I have envied a great many people who led difficult lives and led them well.' "*—Theodore Roosevelt

(Coach Clayton McCullah) "Real men work hard...nuff said."

Yes...enough said.

One of the most important times a guy really needs to "man up" and demonstrate the qualities of a strong Godly man is when he becomes a father. A boy is going to see the examples of what a man is suppose to be by looking at his own dad. Your children often times will take from

you your best qualities and your worst qualities. Every so often I come across a youth who the minute you start talking to them you discover their admiration for their father.

Jacob Miles, or as his friends refer to him as Boo, is one of those youth. His dad was such a strong influence in his life. When I asked Boo to sit down at my computer and write about his dad I was shocked when he instantly sat down and started typing…and an hour and a half later was STILLL typing. When Boo finished his first words to me were, "I could have written even more."

My father is and always will be the closest person to me. I am by definition a "Daddy's boy." My father has always been my closest friend. As a young kid you could always find me on his hip. He is my hero.

The qualities describing who my father is to me would be endless. He is strong, caring, and compassionate.

For half of my life my father has raised me and my brother by himself. He was going through some very rough times, from his divorce with my mother, to his company going under, to hopping from job to job. We lost our house and were extremely tight on money. For the first few years my father truly didn't know how we would make it month to month. My father was dealing with a lot. As a young teenager I never saw the struggle he was going through. This is why I describe him as a strong person. Not just physically, but mentally and emotionally. My father is the kind of person that when life gets rough he does not falter, but steps up and overcomes. This is one of the biggest things my father has instilled in me. Philippians 4:13, "I can do all things through Christ who strengthens me," was something my father always told me. When my backs against the wall I was taught to step up and overcome adversity. My father taught me what it's like to be a strong individual physically, mentally and emotionally.

As I started to get into my mid to late teens I started to see life more clearly. I started to notice the struggles my family was going through. On top of that I was now starting to experience life such as dating, friendships, tougher schooling and sports. I was starting to experience things I've never felt before like heartbreak, rejection, and bullying. I didn't have any idea how to handle these things. I sought comfort in my father. My father is a Godly man and taught me to seek Christ. My father would preach to me a lot. When I was 13, I went through one of the hardest times of my life. My first true love broke up with me. But this wasn't the only thing. Like I said before, my father was raising me so my mother wasn't around much. When she was she would be horrible to me. During that time, mom had recently crushed me and then my girlfriend broke up with me. My heart was a wreck. I suffered with very bad depression and tried to take my own life but failed. Soon after that I was saved. My father is the main reason I came to find Christ and could possibly be the reason I am still alive today. My father is the most compassionate and loving man I know. I go to him for everything. Even my friends go to him and look to him as a father. He's actually not just my dad, but a dad to a lot of others.

Some of the most important things my father has influenced me in my life would be schooling, sports, career choice, and how to be a man. First, I am an honor student and was graduated from high school at the top of my class. My father made sure school came first in my life. I wanted to be a pro athlete, but my father told me, "I want my son to own the team, not play on it." So, I made grades a top priority. Next, my father was an elite athlete so I looked to him my whole life as not only a dad but a coach. My dad has coached me in every sport I've played my entire life. Not only did he teach me how to play the sport but he taught me how to be a coach. I took his coaching style and philosophy and use them now as I coach my wrestling team. My dad was a passionate coach that was strictly business but was also like a father to the kids he coached. Still, to this day, my father is called coach.

My father was an excellent salesman for the majority of his life. Mostly because he has phe-nomenal social skills and can talk to people very well. My father passed that on to me and I must say I am extremely outgoing and it's very easy for me to talk to just about anyone. I'm by no means a shy person either. I love meeting new people. Now my father runs a finance company. He has influenced me to pursue accounting and finance and make that a profession. I love my major and truly believe it's the best fit for me.

The single greatest thing my father has ever taught me is how to be a man. There are so many aspects to it and so many of those aspects only a man can teach. One thing would be how to be a great father. My father is the greatest example of an excellent father. He is my best friend. He is the person I will always seek guidance from. Also, he is strict and accepts nothing but my best. He pushes me to strive to be a better man daily in life, sports, school and much more. He taught me that anything I do, I do my best or I'm just wasting my God given talent. Lastly, my dad has taught me how to be a great role model for society and how to be a great role model for those who are younger. I do all I can for the youth because I know how important an older man is to young people, especially boys. Some kids lack a good father figure and my father always stepped into that role for those kids. I do all I can to do the same because I know how lucky I was to have a great dad.

Some of the major areas my dad taught me in were hard work, humbleness and faithfulness.

Since my dad has been my coach my entire life he pushed me to do my best in everything I did. I watched how hard my dad worked, even when times were tough, and that taught me to persevere and overcome. There's nothing I can't achieve because I know God has my back.

My dad always preached to me about being humble. He always told me actions speak louder than words. I wasn't taught to talk trash but out-work others, so others would see it. Talk is cheap if you can't back it up. I was taught to keep my focus, get my business done, and keep my mouth shut. Ignorant people try to use words to prove themselves. Smart people just do it.

I remember how my father taught me about faithfulness. My girlfriend cheated on me and he told me to let it go. Of course I didn't want to, but he told me this is why you want to be faithful; to make sure you never make someone ever feel the hurt you feel. This brings me to the next thing he taught me. He taught me to do everything I can possibly do to make everyone around me feel joyful. He taught me to not hurt people intentionally. Of course, I would hurt people on accident, but he taught me about forgiveness for not only giving it but getting it. I can only say I'm a very sweet guy because I strive to please others as much as possible.

All in all, my dad has the largest influence over anyone else in my life. He has taught me almost everything I know and has helped me become who I am today. I am so thankful that God honored me with such a phenomenal father! I owe everything to him; my call into ministry, my accomplishments in school, my achievements in sports, my career choice, and most of all how to be a better, godly, and compassionate man. He is the biggest and greatest influence in my life. I would not be anything without him.

(Coach Lance Roweton) "Work hard for your money, and make your money work hard for you. Invest all you can at an early age. It will pay off in the long run. When thinking about your money situation, think about income streams. What are you doing that brings money your way? Some people have one source of income that is so large that one source is all they need. If you are lucky enough to have one of those jobs, God bless you! If you are not so lucky, don't be afraid to do things on the side that creates another stream of income. Don't spend more than you make. Be careful when using credit cards. If you must use one, make sure you can pay it off in a short time...preferably that month. Failure to plan is planning to fail. Set goals for yourself and plan to achieve those goals. Realize that everything you do in your life has consequences...both positive and negative. Follow through with your plan. Be a finisher throughout your life. When things get tough, set your eye on the prize and keep going forward toward that goal."

Successful people don't give up when the going gets tough. They dig in and work harder to succeed. We have become a lazy, instant, society that has forgotten the satisfaction of working hard for what we want. Instead, we take out loans, go in debt, file bankruptcy and rely on the government to pay our way in life.

If you want something, then work and save for it. This actually works well!

(Kwasi Ofori-Yeboah) "An athlete appreciates the value and importance of hard work. Not many people see all the hours, sweat and toil they put into their sport, and yet they are able to witness the pay off when they compete. The same is true in life. There is a saying that 'nothing good comes easy.' In other words, you must work hard at your goals in life if you want to succeed. Failure is not an option, so keep up the hard work and success will greet your efforts. Don't ever quit on yourself. Always work hard at whatever you do."

Elgin's Story

Some people have a way of sneaking into your life and becoming a very special part of it. A few years ago,

Elgin and Bailey

when I first met Elgin, I knew there was something great about him. Elgin became good friends with my daughters (it helps to build your youth group whenever you have beautiful daughters). There were times when things would get a little rocky between them. You see, Elgin came from quite a different background than my daughters did. But he has always remained faithful and loyal toward my family in the long run. Although his life was not easy, you never heard him complaining about it. Actually, you hardly ever heard him say anything negative about his life. Elgin did not like to take handouts from anyone and always believed in working and earning what was given to him. In High school he was active in sports, kept a high GPA and worked long hours at a job in order to have the things he wanted. But let's start closer to the beginning of Elgin's story so you can see what a truly amazing guy he really is.

When Elgin was three years old, he and his brother went to visit his grandparents who happened to raise mountain lions. The following is Elgin's description of what happened to him that day:

> Well, I was three and my older brother was chasing me in one of those little Flintstone like cars with the yellow top and red bottom every little kid has had one! And I slipped on the sidewalk next to

the cage on little rocks and slid under the cage or close and it grabbed my foot and dragged me under. I don't know how far I slid but while that was happening my brother was SCREAMING bloody murder and all the adults, including my dad, came out and dragged me out from under. I think the lion was occupied with my shoe at that time. After that I was in and out of consciousness. The last thing I remember before waking up in the hospital was being in a car being driven to the hospital. They kept telling me to keep my foot on the dash because I had been bitten there.

Elgin's small little body had been mauled badly by a mountain lion. Elgin had multiple bites all over his body and spent several weeks in critical condition. His family was not sure what the extent of damage was. Elgin pulled through with no permanent damage, but was left with some very nasty looking scars.

When I look at Elgin's life and all he has endured I realize from such a young age what a tough guy he really is and the scars he has lived with, both visible and hidden.

I never really knew my dad. Never got to spend a lot of time with him and I would say he had absolutely no influence on me growing up. My mom had a friend she knew, while growing up, named Danny. Danny and my Grandfather were my male role models. Danny was a great guy who would pick my brother and me up on the weekends and take us places like to the races or a Monster Truck rally whenever there was one near. My Grandfather has had the most influence in my life in the aspect of what kind of man I strive to be, and he's just always been there for me.

I don't really like to judge myself, but I'd say I'm very protective, and, I work to improve myself mentally and physically. As a teenager I was very rebellious and I hated being told what to do. I'd get into trouble occasionally but nothing too serious. I maintained a good GPA throughout high school but I never went the extra mile in the classroom.

Some of the best memories I had as a teenager were all the crazy, fun things I did with the Martin family and going to Super Summer (youth camp). I also liked hanging out with my friends Randy, David, Alex, and Brandon.

The previous statements were pretty much all Elgin had to say about his life. I know there's a lot more to it though. Elgin has had to endure so much more than what most typical teenagers ever have to. He had a choice to make though. He could have felt sorry for himself that so many bad things happened to him in life and wallowed in self pity. He could have decided to take the easy way out and use the sympathy from others in order to get the things he wanted in life. But he didn't. Instead, Elgin did something that is becoming a rarity in this day and age. He worked hard.

Today I'm so happy to know that the protectiveness Elgin has in his heart and the hard work instilled into his character is part of what keeps America safe.

Elgin graduated from high school and became a part of The Few. The Proud. The Marines. I couldn't be more happier for you Elgin! Ooh Rah!!

"War is an ugly thing, but it is not the ugliest of things. The decayed and degraded state of moral and patriotic feeling which thinks that nothing is worth war is much worse. A man who has nothing for which he is willing to fight, nothing he cares about more than his own personal safety, is a miserable creature who has no chance of being free, unless made so by the exertions of better men than himself."

— John Stuart Mill

This seems to be a main theme throughout this book: You are responsible for yourself. If you want to succeed then work hard at all you do and don't take the easy way out. Make no excuses and be patient. We get so impatient when striving for our goals that we tend to lower our standards. Don't do this. Ever! There is no need.

If you want to fail then be lazy, make excuses, and watch others get ahead of you. That's pretty simple.

(Griff Schoen) "My dad always told me, 'If It's worth doing, it's worth doing right. So do it right the first time.' Nothing in this life is free. Everything takes hard work. Whether it's your job, your family, or your marriage, you can't coast along and expect everything to go your way."

If it's worth doing, it's worth doing right. These are wise words. Take your time and do something right. It will be noticed. Doing things just for the money has short-term benefits. You'll have more money. That's it. The contentment is short-lived. If you're going to do something for a long period of time, your heart has to be in it or you're going to be miserable. Working hard sometimes seems futile. Be persistent in your hard work. It does pay off in the long haul. Don't cut corners or take short cuts in your work or in your studies. Don't just do what is easy. Try hard. Do that which is hard. It does eventually get noticed and does produce results.

(Coach Daniel Bayless) "I know a lot of talented, gifted men who don't work hard. For the most part, they haven't made anything of their lives. I also know many people without talent or a wonderful gift, but the drive to work hard. Every one of them has made something of themselves."

"Laziness leads to poverty; hard work makes you rich" (Proverbs 10:4).

(Marca Deimund) "Work as hard when your boss is not around as you do when he's standing right next to you. Bosses are intelligent people. They can see what was done when they left, and what was accomplished when they return. Resist the urge to work like 'everyone' else! Work harder – do not drop to the status quo, but raise the bar for everyone else. It is very hard to see those who don't work as hard get raises and promotions when you get overlooked, but this is where you win! Colossians 3:22 says, 'Slaves, in all things obey those who are your masters on earth, not with external service, as those who merely please men, but with sincerity of heart, fearing the Lord. Whatever you do, do your work heartily, as for the Lord rather than for men; know that from the Lord you will receive the reward of the inheritance. It is the Lord Christ whom you serve.'

(Barry Farr) "I want to encourage you to keep working hard in everything you do. If you are a hard worker you will stand out in our culture. Many people do not know how or choose not to work hard any more. As a business owner I can assure you that I consider it a real blessing to find an employee who is hard working. Hard work will bring you good things. Do not forget that it took hard work to succeed and will take hard work to continue to succeed!"

"For even when we were with you, we would give you this command; If anyone is not willing to work, let him not eat. For we hear that some among you walk in idleness, not busy at work, but busybodies. Now such persons we command and encourage in the Lord Jesus Christ to do their work quietly and to earn their own living" (2 Thessalonians 3:10-12).

Real Men work hard.

Chapter 13

BUYING A CAR

"Speaking to the people, he went on, 'Take care! Protect yourself against the least bit of greed. Life is not defined by what you have, even when you have a lot" (Luke 12:15 MSG).

(Coach Daniel Bayless) "Save up your money first and buy it second. It will cost you much less this way. Never borrow money on anything that depreciates."

My dad always said to never buy a new car because it loses its value the minute you drive it off the lot.

Take your time when looking for a car. I know this is a pretty exciting time but you want to make sure you get the best for your money. Your first car does not have to be anything fancy. The main purpose of a car is to get you from point A to point B using as little gas as possible!

If you find a car you like then do your research on it. Look and see if it's dependable or if it's known to have problems. Ask the owner if you can take it to a garage to be checked out. Don't be afraid to ask questions! This is a big purchase and one you will probably have for a while. Be smart with your purchase.

(Kwasi Ofori-Yeboah) "Buying a car is fun, but comes with a lot of responsibility. It is important therefore to take certain things into consideration before you make the decision to buy a car. First of all, you want to buy a car that you can afford (sounds simple enough, but let me elaborate). Sometimes people make the decision to buy a car based on emotional rather than rational calculation. So they wind up buying something that eventually becomes a drag on their finances and their life in general. Keep in mind that in addition to the monthly payments (unless you paid cash for the car, which will be awesome if you are able to do that), you will pay insurance, as well the cost of maintenance. In other words, car ownership will add a monthly expense to your bill, and that is why you want to make sure that you can afford the purchase. Whether you buy new or used depends on your circumstances, your finances and your preferences, but most experts advise against buying a new car. While it will give you the peace of mind of not breaking down soon and not worrying about expensive repairs, it will also quickly depreciate in value as soon as you drive it off the lot. They advise that you buy a fairly good used one. The payments will be more affordable and you will get a reliable vehicle for at least a few years. Hopefully by the time it reaches the stage where major repairs might start creeping up, you will be in a position to get another one. The point is this; you will want to be practical when it comes to buying a car. Use your head and not your heart. Go for functionality-something decent that will get you from point A to point B and not something in vogue (the latest car) which will cost you an arm and a leg and drain you. You simply don't want to stress about car payments. There are decent cars out there which are affordable and those are the ones you should be considering and not those that make a "fashion" or a "status" statement, but lead to financial headaches."

If you can't afford the gas, tags, insurance, and maintenance on a car, then don't get one. There are many other ways of getting around. I know that's not the cool thing to do but it's the smart thing. Most places have buses; you can carpool with someone, ride a bike, or walk. Don't get yourself in financial trouble over a car. It's just not worth it.

(Coach Lance Roweton) "When buying a car don't be afraid to look at a good used vehicle. When you buy a new vehicle it loses about a third of its value when you drive it off the lot. The upside with buying new is the terms they give you are better. A lot of dealers will give you 0% interest when buying a new vehicle. Calculate it out and see how much you will actually pay for each vehicle and then do what you want. Either way; drive your vehicle as long as you can. I have had my vehicle paid off for about 7 years, and it is nice not to have that payment."

Having a car should not be a status symbol. You don't have to have a new or different car every other year. Drive it for as long as you can. Usually when it starts costing more in repairs than its worth is when you need to start looking for a different one.

(Papa & Granny) "When you buy your first car,

just know it is a big responsibility. It is not something that you just get into and drive. You have insurance, car tags, tires to buy, gas oil, and belts to keep up and a motor. Be proud of it. Keep it nice. It is not to be raced but to keep the speed limit."

Having a car is a privilege and a big responsibility. Take care of it. Keep it clean first off. Maintenance is a must if you want your car to last. Make sure you are getting the oil changed and the tires checked regularly. Find a good mechanic whom you can trust and they will help you take care of your car.

Don't be stupid when driving your car. Laws are made to keep everyone safe. Don't get in your car if you're angry or upset. Don't be distracted in any way. The speed limit is there for a purpose. I would rather you arrive somewhere late then not at all. Slow down and obey the signs. There are many other drivers on the road and their lives have value. Respect that.

(Barry Farr) "I do not have much to say about buying a car except to tell you what I do. I depend on the expertise of others who know more about cars."

If you don't know what to look for or do when it's time to buy a car don't be afraid to ask someone who does to go along with you. There is a great deal to know when buying a car.

Chapter 14

BUYING A HOME

"It takes wisdom to build a house, and understanding to set it on firm foundation; It takes knowledge to furnish its rooms with fine furniture and beautiful draperies" (Proverbs 24: 3, 4 MSG).

(Gina Green) "Live within your means. Figure your debt to income ratio before you get a loan. (45%= DANGER!)"

Buying a house is exciting and overwhelming. There is so much to consider. Before you even start to look at houses, figure out what you can afford. You need to consider your income, your savings, and your debt.

(Coach Lance Roweton) "In the next 10 years you will buy a car and maybe a house. These are both big ticket items. Negotiate the best price you can get as well as the best terms when buying either. Try to get an interest rate that is low and locked in for the life of the loan. Do not stretch yourself financially with either of these purchases.

Get something that you can be proud of and that you can afford without being on the edge of not making it. When buying a home, make sure you are going to be there at least 3 years before you buy. If you can't say that for sure then rent."

Most people start out renting. Even if you're just renting a home this is still your home. Keep it nice. It is a reflection of you and your family. So whether you are renting or buying a house, there is work to be done. Don't be lazy. You are being blessed with a gift from God. Not keeping your home up is like taking that gift and crumpling it up and throwing it on the floor.

Keep the yard mowed and the flowerbeds clean. Make sure the roof and gutters are in good shape and the paint is not peeling. Keep your yard weed free. Your neighbors will appreciate your efforts. On the inside, keep things picked up and kept clean. A strange thing happens with homes. They take on the scent of the family that lives there. I've had people walk into my house and smile and say, "This smells like you." It's true though. The scents you have around your house cling to you. If you have a filthy house with dirty laundry everywhere, dishes piled in the sink, and a floor that hasn't seen a vacuum in ages you are just being lazy.

Things go wrong with houses. Toilets clog, hot water heaters go out, oven's stop heating, air conditioners stop cooling. Make sure you have money set aside for home emergencies.

(Kwasi Ofori-Yeboah) "Home ownership is going to mark another important milestone in your life and you should approach it with much thought and care. It is going to be one of the most expensive purchases and investments that you will ever make so proceed with extra caution. One key consideration is location. You don't want to buy a house in a location with a lot of problems, so location is very important. Other than that, you also want to make sure that you are not seduced by the bells and whistles, which can drive up the cost of a house. You want comfortable house payments, which means you must buy a house where the payments (mortgage, insurance, taxes) do not consume more than 25% of your gross income (the experts typically put that figure at 30% but I think 25% is more realistic). Remember that in addition to the monthly payments, you have to make allowance for home maintenance expenses and other bills such as utilities. The one mistake that you surely want to avoid is buying a house and becoming 'house poor.' That is, paying so much in house payment that you literally have no money to do anything else, like go on vacation, etc. Another reason to avoid a pricey house is that the financial strain could be a severe handicap on your lifestyle as well as on your relationship. You don't want money and the pursuit of it or the lack of it to dominate your life and one way to avoid that trap is buy a well-priced house where the monthly payments and expenses are less than 25% of what you make. Sometimes people make the mistake of buying a house based on their projected earnings. So they buy more than they can afford now with the hope that with time, their income will rise so as to make the payments more manageable. Don't go that route in your decision making about buying a house. What if your earnings don't rise as expected or what if your circumstances change and your income drops? Home ownership has a lot of benefits and at the appropriate time, you should consider being a home owner. But keep in mind the advice above before purchasing a house."

When you buy a house don't let it consume you. If you stay within your means then you will have money and time for other things.

The day you buy your first home will be a day you feel truly accomplished. Don't rush this at all. Find a realtor you like and are comfortable with and trust. Take as much time as you need looking at different houses in different locations. When you find one you like don't make a decision that day. Wait at least a day. Give it a lot of thought and make sure you can afford it. Never buy a house spontaneously.

(Coach Daniel Bayless) "Start SMALL. Most of the time it is best to first rent a home. A person can learn a lot about owning a house through renting. With renting there is no home insurance and no taxes. Of course, the down side is your rent money only buys you time instead of investing in yourself. If you are willing to work hard, a first house that is a small fixer upper is a great investment. Buy it and fix it up and live in it for three years, so you don't have to pay capital gains tax when you sell it for a big profit. Then you can move to something a little nicer and repeat the process. This formula worked for me. I rented while I saved my money for my first house which I bought with cash. It was very small, 740 sq. ft., on a little lot and needed some improvement. I sold it four years later for a big profit and got a bigger house that needed a lot of work on a corner lot in a nice neighborhood. I was able to buy it with cash too. Now we live in a

3500 sq. ft. dream house on forty acres and it is all paid for. But we were only able to do this because we started small."

A bigger house does not always mean a better life. Some of the best times you will have will be in that little tiny rental house you made into a home.

(Barry Farr) "I would encourage you to buy a home because it is a true symbol of freedom. In many countries the average person does not own his living space. Typically a few own the actual property. It is a huge responsibility, but it is worth it."

It's a crazy feeling of accomplishment when a realtor hands you a set of keys to your home. It's yours; no one else's. You've worked hard and saved and now you own your own home.

The fears of the past are put to rest. Growing up, you were moved from place to place never really knowing where your true home was. Hotels, cars, and dirty run down rentals, and trailers infested with roaches were where you stayed. But now, you have your own home. Take pride in it. Then give it over to God and open up your home to others.

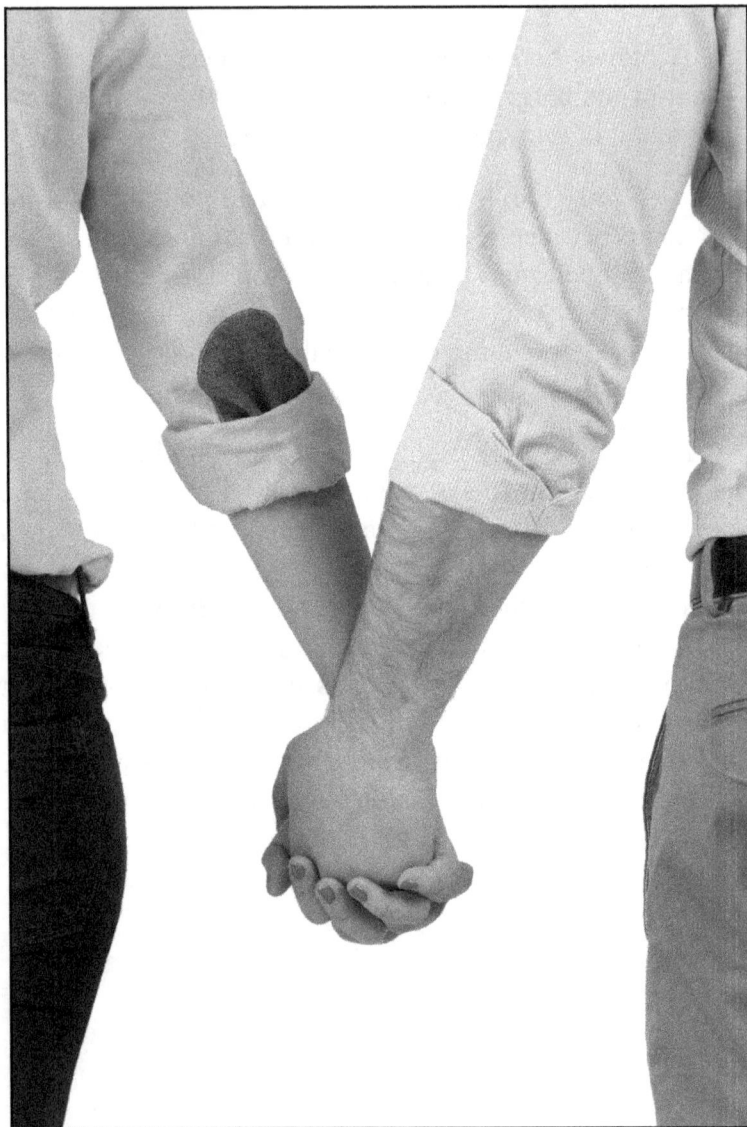

Chapter 15

MARRIAGE

"Many a man claims to have unfailing love, but a faithful man who can find? The righteous man leads a blameless life; blessed are his children after him" (Proverbs 20:6-7).

Walter Wangerin wrote, "Love lies a little. Love, the desire to like and to be liked, feels so good when it is satisfied that it never wants to stop. Therefore, love edits the facts in order to continue to feel good...Love idealized both of us."[1]

(Papa & Granny) "Pray that God will send you the lady He wants you to spend your life with. Remember, marriage is a 50/50 giving and receiving. You treat each other with lots of love and respect. Do not go to bed without telling her you love her. Thank her for little things she does. Just remember to enjoy being together doing nothing. Above all be faithful to her."

When you have been courting or dating awhile, sooner or later you will start to ask yourself, "Is this the one?" Don't just base your answers on feelings. Feelings can change. Put your relationship to the test! If you are serious about wanting to find that wife, who you want to spend the rest of your life with, then take your time and really make sure this relationship is what you want.

You need to make sure you're compatible. More of your time as a married couple will take place in Walmart then in the bedroom. You need to make sure you can enjoy doing every day errands together. If your relationship is always in "romantic date mode" you're not ready to marry. Life isn't always about romance. Sometimes it's about picking out toilet paper at the local store.

Keith R. Anderson wrote a small book called, Is this the One? I highly recommend it to anyone before they marry, and will refer to it multiple times during this chapter. His tests are simple and very insightful. In his book he gives nine tests for Marriage.

Test one is The Builder's Square Test. This is similar to what I just shared with you. He states, "In our society much of marriage is spent in the car; it is lived out in mundane dailyness. The grand events of weddings, commencements and birthdays are the exception. Marriage is lived 'on the way'-running errands, doing chores, cleaning the house and balancing the checkbook. You need not delight in every one of these tasks, but the Builder's Square Test wants to know: do you delight in spending time with each other-even common, ordinary, everyday time?"[2]

(Coach Lance Roweton) "Ask her father if you can marry her before you ask her. That is the respectful thing to do. I can tell you, my daughters will not get married without Daddy's approval! When you choose a wife, be choosey. You need to find someone you are friends with and that you can talk to. If you only marry for looks you will be in trouble. Looks fade with age and so will the relationship if that is what your relationship is based on. You need to pay attention to her family, as you will be marrying her and her family. Never forget the girl you fell in love with. Marriage will have ups and downs but the down times won't quite be so down if you can still see that beautiful girl you fell in love with. In any relationship...especially the relationship with your wife...don't worry about being right. Try to make her happy while maintaining your own happiness. If she does the same, your marriage will be a good one."

When you got up this morning, and looked in the mirror, the sight you saw probably was not pretty! Your hair more than likely was sticking up. Your breath might have smelled like something crawled in your mouth and died while you were sleeping. That's reality. You don't look your best.

Don't marry someone until you have seen each other at both your best and worst.

When preparing for a date with someone, I know girls spend HOURS primping and getting ready. They shower with all kinds of pretty smelling soaps. They shave their legs (something that might not occur on a regular basis after marriage. They make their skin all smooth and soft with lotion. Several kinds of hair products are applied while blow drying and curling and straightening. The decision has to be made whether to wear their hair down long and flowing or pinned up so their necks look long and graceful. Then the face paint comes out and another hour is spent carefully applying just the right shades of color to make their eyes look bigger and their lips look kissable and all imperfections covered up. After all that, much time is spent pulling one outfit after another from the closet to see which one will make them look the closest to perfection. When they step in front of you...ta da!! She's the most beautiful thing you have ever seen and life is great! But... have you seen her with a runny nose, and her eyes all puffy and red, whining because she has the flu? Or curled up on the couch with a heating pad across her stomach, random food items surrounding her (mainly consisting of chocolate) snarling when she talks to you with an, "I could kill you" look in her eyes. Yes, the dreaded "that time of the month." In other words, have you spent enough time together that you have seen each other fully and truly how you really are.

Keith Anderson again quotes, "Disillusionment is a good idea for a couple! When you become disillusioned, you set your illusions aside. When a person travels across the vast wasteland of a desert, he begins to imagine that he sees what he wants most at the moment-water. Dating is not that different for some. You begin to fantasize that she is exactly what you want most at that moment. The trouble with a mirage is that it is not real. When you get to your destination you discover that it is only more of the same. That is why disillusionment may be a good idea...If marriage is based on the illusion of perfection; you will be greatly and quickly disappointed."

You have to see who she really is and you must allow her to know you as you truly are. Both of you must understand each other's standards and values. Know each other's habits and the things each likes and doesn't like. Remember, you cannot force someone to change. How they are as a single person will be how they are as a married person, so make sure you really know how they truly are before you tie the knot! This does not in any way mean move in together! Big, big mistake! Don't "play house." The only time you should live together is after you become husband and wife. Don't devalue marriage by "trying it out" first to see if it will work.

(Gina Green) "Find a woman who does not need to be rescued. She needs to be whole and happy before she starts dating you. You cannot make someone else happy, because happiness comes from within. You cannot save a woman who has major problems that she cannot solve herself. Don't marry a woman unless the way things are when you are dating makes you so incredibly happy that you want to live with her forever without changing anything about her or you or the relationship. Don't marry a woman thinking that it will change a major problem. It won't. It will only get worse. Consider waiting until you are 25 to get married. Remember, marriage is PERMANENT! Forever! Choose wisely."

"The two will become one flesh" (Genesis 2:24). God's math is a little different than ours. He takes 1+1 and it comes out to equal one. One whole person plus another whole person get married and they become one through God in spirit and love. What He doesn't do is take $\frac{1}{2}$ + $\frac{1}{2}$ = 1. Don't go into marriage thinking this woman will mend the broken pieces in you or that you can "fix" what's broken within her. Two broken people, when they come together, are still broken. In a marriage, you bring both everything that is good in each other and everything that is not so great. If there is dysfunction it will still be there when you marry. Marriage isn't a magical spell like the movies portray it to be.

Bill and Lynne Hybels wrote,

"In most cases, an unhappy single person will be an unhappy married person. A bitter, angry single person will be a bitter angry married person... Marriage does not produce life or character transformations. Such changes are produced by the inner work of the Holy Spirit which is not dependent on one's marital status."[3]

You have got to work on your own self and make sure you would want to be the kind of person you yourself would want to marry. Examine your life and your character. With God's help, fix what you think is broken. If you feel you cannot be whole or secure or stable unless you are constantly seeking the attention of a female than you are not ready to marry. You have GOT to learn to stand alone on your own two feet in life before uniting with someone else. Do not marry someone to fill some sort of emotional need; either yours or hers. Work on your own personal growth. Don't depend on someone else to work on it for you.

It seems in today's world, marriage is done on a trial basis. Society tells us to "try each other out" before making it legal, or, go ahead and get married, have a big party, play house and when things get a bit rough or you grow bored with each other just call it quits and move on to the next someone.

This is not how marriage is intended to be. A real man of integrity will honor marriage. He will take his time and not rush into it.

A good piece of advice is given by Keith Anderson from test seven: The Day-timer Test, "Nothing tests the potential of a relationship like time. Take out your calendar and write down the date you became certain that she was the one. If you are still certain twelve months from now, then go slow and give it some more time. What do you have to lose? If 'she' is the one for you, then you will have a year to develop your friendship, trust, loyalty, communication, companionship and love. If she's the one for you and you nourish your love carefully for a year, the rewards will be great."

(Kwasi Ofori-Yeboah) "Other than a relationship with God, perhaps one of the most important decisions you will make will be marrying the woman of your dreams. But first you must find this woman before you can marry her. So how do you find her? Well, it begins with the dating process, a very necessary step. You simply don't want to marry someone you don't know well enough, that is too risky, because of all the unknowns and how that might invariably ruin the relationship.

So you want to start by some self-introspection. Ask yourself; 'what do I want in a woman? What kind of woman do I want to share the rest of my life with? What are the absolutely important qualities that my future wife should have?' Mind you, you will not have an answer to all these questions now and probably never will, but at least it is important to be clear-eyed when entering into a relationship, especially one with the potential for a long-term commitment.

You definitely want to talk to some older folks and ask for their views on marriage. Experience, they say, is the best teacher. Those who have traveled the road before can tell you about the bumps and curves on the road, and how to negotiate them... It all begins with finding the right person, as a bad marriage could scuttle your plans for the future. The one thing you don't want to do when it comes to marriage is to rush into it. The stakes are high and you want to do your homework by addressing some of the questions raised earlier about your expectations of your partner, etc. As enriching, rewarding and as vital as marriage could be, it is not without its ups and downs.

How you resolve these difficulties will depend largely on the foundations upon which the marriage is built. Mutual trust, love and respect coupled with God's grace will go a long way to building a solid relationship. And remember, nothing good comes easy. So you will have to work at your marriage to ensure success. Don't take your partner for granted and don't take the marriage for granted. Work hard at it and you will ensure the fruits of your labor with a contented life and a blessed family."

Is the woman you want to marry your best friend? If not, don't marry her. Don't get two steps ahead of yourself. Start out as friends, then best friends. Look at the characteristics of a good friend: they give you their time and attention, they are very loyal and honest (even when they know the truth might hurt you), they stick up for you, they accept you for who you are, they forgive you, they understand you even when you don't understand yourself, they lift you up not pull you down. Is this woman you are considering marrying really your best friend? If not, don't get married.

(Griff Schoen) Of marriages today, 50% end in divorce. If you don't want to be a statistic, then take your time finding a good woman. Don't marry the first one that comes along. Once you find a good one, treat her like a princess.

Believe it or not there is more to marriage than sex. Usually when people try to justify why they are living together it's really more about convenient sex. Don't put yourself in that situation. If you truly love this woman, then wait. Don't move in together. Think about something you had to wait a long time for in order to have? When you finally got it you appreciated it so much more. You cherished it, and wanted to take good care of it.

If you're having pregnancy scares before you say I do, then more than likely you have placed far too much importance on sex in your relationship. If neither one of you can control yourselves concerning sex before your married this is a problem. Think about it. Technically, you're not married yet so you are already cheating on your future spouse. If it was that easy for both of you to cheat then it could very well be that easy for one of you to cheat after saying "I do." It's all about disciplining yourselves. Again, if it's something worth waiting for then wait. Stop giving another little piece of yourself that was meant just for your wife to someone else. She doesn't deserve that. If the woman you are considering marrying looks at sex as something casual, then you better really think twice about this relationship. You may be receiving more than just a wedding band. Today there are over 25 major sexually transmitted diseases out there. The HPV (Human Papilloma Virus) has anywhere from 80 – 100 different strains. The ONLY way to be completely free from STDs is to be completely 100% abstinent. That means absolutely nothing from the very top of your head to the tips of your toes tips should be in someone else's undies zone and nothing of theirs should be in your undies zone. You can get some STD's by simply coming in contact with someone's undies zone (i.e. HPV & Herpes). The only way you can be sure you're not getting or passing on a disease is to be 100% abstinent. Marry someone who is not infected and who has saved themselves just for their husband, and then be faithful to your spouse.

Anderson says in his test number six labeled The EPT Test, "If you have become sexually active in your serious relationship, back off and abstain from sex for thirty days. Then talk about your relationship. If you can't refrain from sex, I believe your marriage will head for failure, because it is based on physical gratification and sexual pleasure rather than on love and integrity.

(Coach Daniel Bayless) "Anyone who says 'looks don't matter' is a fool or a liar. Looks mean everything. Some women look beautiful on the outside, some on the inside, some both, some neither. Just remember you will be with your wife for the rest of your life and after time a woman's outward appearance fades while her inward looks are more noticeable every day."

"Charm can fool you. Beauty fades, but a woman who has respect for the LORD should be praised" (Proverbs 31:30).

Don't rush in order to marry what you think "looks" good or "feels" right. Wait, and make sure she is the role model you want your future family to represent. Test five in Anderson's book is called the Truth or Dare test. Keith states, "Truth-telling is an essential building block for a successful relationship. I suggest that you use a very simple tool to measure this quality in a potential mate; if she says she will do something, can you count on its being done-and not just at her convenience? This will give you great insight into her integrity and sincerity....The Latin word for 'sincere' is a combination of two other words: without wax. When an artisan made a clay pot, he would fire it in a kiln to make it solid. The process of heating the clay would sometimes create a hairline crack in the pot, invisible to the casual observer. When the pot was painted, the crack would become visible and the price would be reduced. So an unscrupulous artisan would fill the crack with wax, making it difficult to detect. Yet in the sunlight, a careful consumer could see that the pot contained a flaw, a crack, which would later cause the piece to shatter.

At its most elemental level, marriage is a promise. It's sincere-without wax; no fillers, no excuses, the real thing, the truth. Marriage is a covenant of trust between two people...Marry someone who loves you enough to tell you the truth-all the time-in things little and big. Marry someone who cares more about the sunlight that the wax."

(Stephanie Schraeder) "She is still someone's daughter and someone's princess. Now she is your Queen. Date your wife, hug her, hold her hand, kiss her forehead, hand, and cheek. Tell her several times a day, in some way, how much she means to you. Tell her every single night, "I love you."

The rings are on the fingers and the "I do's" have been said. Promises to have and to hold from this day forward, for better or for worse, for richer, for poorer, in sickness and in health, to love and to cherish; from this day forward until death do you part have been made. You are now someone's husband. Now what? Some of the absolute best advice on how a husband and wife should be comes from God's word.

"Wives, understand and support your husbands in ways that show your support for Christ. The husband provides leadership to his wife the way Christ does to his church, not by domineering but by cherishing. So just as the church submits to Christ as he exercises such leadership, wives should likewise submit to their husbands. Husbands, go all out in your love for your wives, exactly as Christ did for the church – a love marked by giving, not getting. Christ's love makes the church whole. His words evoke her beauty. Everything he does and says is designed to bring the best out of her, dressing her in dazzling white silk, radiant with holiness. And that is how husbands ought to love their wives. They're really doing themselves a favor – since they're already 'one' in marriage. No one abuses his own body, does he? No, he feeds and pampers it. That's how Christ treats us, the church, since we are a part of his body. And this is why a man leaves his father and mother and cherishes his wife. No longer two, they become 'one flesh.' This is a huge mystery, and I don't pretend to understand it all. What is clearest to me is the way Christ treats the church. And this provides a good picture of how each husband is to treat his wife, loving himself in loving her, and how each wife is to honor her husband" (Ephesians 5:22-33 MSG).

Your wife should never doubt in anyway how much you love her. Make sure you both show her and tell her often. Never assume she knows. Don't just compliment her on her looks or her body. Those things can be gone in an instant. If she thinks the only thing that attracts her to you is her physical qualities then God forbid something happens that disfigures her in some way, no amount of words from you will make her believe she is beautiful in your eyes. Make sure you are complimenting her on her heart qualities, her character qualities.

Pay attention to her and spend time with her. Believe me, if you don't, there is always someone out there that would be willing to!

Don't smother her though. Let her be the woman God created her to be. Don't try to change her into someone you want her to be. If you want to change her then you probably shouldn't have married her in the first place.

Find things that both of you enjoy doing together as a couple but also make sure you have things that you enjoy doing separately. Too much time together can cause you to grate on each other's nerves. It's OK for you to have your guy friends to go do guy things with and for her to have her women friends. Women are very relational. They need their friends.

I believe the day and age we live in has made it very easy for people to emotionally cheat on each other. Texting, emailing, IM'ing gives instant private access to anyone. There's even websites that help married people have affairs! So how do you prevent this from invading your marriage? You protect it in love. I'm not talking about trying to control every little move your wife makes. If you have to play detective in your marriage then your marriage is in serious trouble because the trust has left. Never give your wife a reason to doubt you. Be honest in your marriage.

Fight for your wife not with her. All marriages go through rough times. It's how you handle these times that can make or break a marriage. Know when to humble yourself and say you're sorry.

You are to be the leader in your home. That's the way God intended marriage to be. This again should not be done in a controlling manner, but in a wise, loving manner. You should be the one making sure your family is taken care of. Work and provide for your family's needs. You should be the one leading your family spiritually. Take them to church weekly. Pray with them daily. Read the Bible with them and study it together. Your family structure should look like this: God as the head of your home, then you the husband, next your wife, and then the children. Your wife is intended to be a helper to you. The two of you should make decisions together with you taking into consideration her input. Ultimately though, the final say should come from you. I know this is not what's popular with the world but it's what's right in God's eyes. The Bible says a wife should show support to her husband and a husband should lead his wife, not by control but by cherishing.

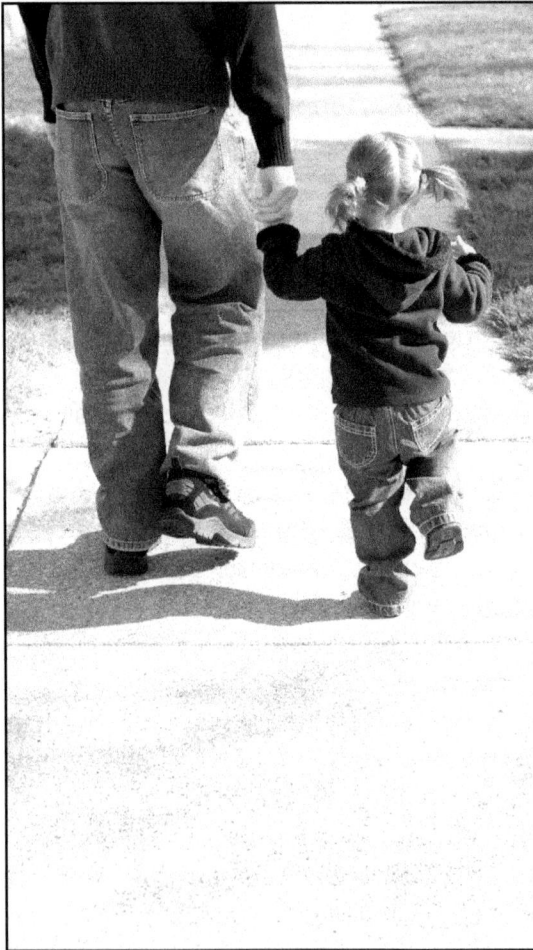

Chapter 16

RAISING CHILDREN

"You shall teach them diligently to your children, and shall talk of them when you sit in your house, and when you walk by the way, and when you lie down, and when you rise" (Deuteronomy 6:7).

(Coach Daniel Bayless) "Express love to your kids every day. Boys need to know when you are proud of them and girls need to know you will always be there for them. Kids read what you do, not what you say; so do right. Discipline is a must but it will lead to rebellion if it is done without love. Also, read to them every night. If you have daughters they have to know they are your princesses and they have to know you love them. Tell them every day; make them sick of hearing it. If you don't show them your love they will go looking for some form of perverted love from someone who will take advantage of their insecurities."

He was known as the worst kid in town, someone who was nothing but trouble. Brandon spent more time in trouble at school, at home, or with the law then he did out of trouble. His reputation went before him. Then one day that all started to change. Sometimes you have to take a peek into the heart of someone to understand why they behave the way they do. In order to do that you must open up your heart a bit to them and take a chance on mixing your life with theirs.

This is Brandon's story.

I thought at times of myself as a low life and a trouble maker. There were times when I wished I was as happy as other people. I actually was jealous. I put on a front at school that I was happy. People had no clue what my home life was really like, and the living "hell" I went through.

My dad had a decent amount of influence on me, mostly bad. He showed me what I didn't want to be like at all. How I refused to treat women and get in my kids face and degrade them because they didn't do good enough or do what I asked them to.

I started drinking at the age of three when my dad had a friend over. My dad poured Captain Morgan and coke in a cup and watched as I climbed up and started drinking it. That was just the beginning of a long line of bad choices on my part.

My dad has been married ten times. One time he went to a bar, got drunk and got married. Drinking was always a problem with my dad. When I was seven we lived in Texas. I had to stop being a kid at that point in order to start taking care of my dad. I constantly had to pick him up off the floor, pick him up off the balcony and even out of the shower whenever he got so drunk he couldn't get up by himself. My dad was married to a woman at that time who was so abusive she actually picked me up by my ears and threw me. There were times I didn't get to go to bed until almost 2 a.m. from having to deal with his drunken stupor and then get myself up at 7 a.m. and go to school.

In my school years I was considered the outcast. I was cool with everyone but never really hung out with anyone. My school friends were just my school friends. I never got to make my school friends my friends outside of school. If I asked my dad if I could go to a football game or just hang out, he always told me no. I was stuck in the house. Because of that I learned a way around it. I would wait until he fell asleep then leave. It got to the point where I would be gone from 10 at night until 5 in the morning.

At the age of 13, I moved to Kansas. It was my seventh grade year. I had to start taking care of my great grandmother. I was skipping school to take care of her and do the things my dad promised he would do. Instead, he sat in the basement in his chair getting drunk. I started doing drugs. I did it because I thought, "Why not, I have nothing else to lose." The only problem was when I came back from being high my problems were 10 times worse.

I also started having sex at the age of 13. No one ever told me it wasn't right. I relied on girls to be that person I felt I could rely on to talk to and make me feel wanted.

My lowest point came when I was 15. I lost my great grandmother that year. At this point I was still drinking and heavily into drugs. I got arrested a few of times, One time for going out with friends and getting drunk, another for driving on a suspended license, and the third for domestic violence. There was a lot of anger in me and I was quick to take it out on whoever crossed me. My life was going downhill fast. If I had one more strike against me at school I would be kicked out. Also, If I had one more strike against me with the law I would go to jail.

I heard from a friend of mine about a youth group in town at the First Baptist Church in Cimarron. I decided I was just going to go and see what it was all about. I got there and felt like it was where I belonged. For a long time I felt like something was missing in my life. I thought it was girls, drugs and alcohol. None of those things filled the sense of belonging that I was looking for. Because of the group I hung around with, I was always in trouble with the law. I knew something was missing, I just didn't know what it was. When I went to church I found the place I fit in. A couple of weeks later one of the happiest memories in my life started taking place. For the first time ever I attended youth camp with my youth group. When I first arrived I was second guessing myself on going. As the week progressed I realized this is what I had been missing. I needed God in my life.

No matter what goes on in your life, it's your choice whether to make it positive or negative. The power is within you. You don't have to believe what everyone else is telling you. It's your choice how you plan your life and which road you want to go down. A great start would be to find a church you feel comfortable with. You don't have to go in there expecting to instantly have a relationship with God, because you're probably not. It's something you grow into. You start as a new born infant. You don't know what you're doing or how to react but as time goes on you grow into your faith. Believe me, if you knew me a few years ago you wouldn't have believed I am who I am today.

To be honest, I didn't even know what being a man really was. I didn't look at when I left home at 17 as being a man or when I graduated college. I didn't see that as being a man. Honestly, I don't think I'm there yet. To me, being a man means taking on responsibilities and having the courage to stand up and do what is right. It also means being humble, patient and Godly. It means understanding and knowing when to back off.

I want to find a Godly woman to start a family with some day, but it's getting harder to do. When I get into a relationship now, I'm not interested in sex. I can do without that. I refuse to have a relationship now based on sex. I want to take my time and find a woman who loves God first and most of all. I'm wanting to find a woman who isn't ashamed of her faith and will share her beliefs. Someone who is strong willed and won't give into peer pressure. I think it's really important to take your time finding the right women. I consider marriage as something sacred. I want to get married once and only once. I bounced back and forth between my parents and learned what marriage was about by stories other people told me.

I learned the important things in life by trial and error and by some positive role models: A man everyone calls Papa (Glenn Walton), my pastor, Richard Diamund, and my Uncle Jeff.

One thing my uncle would always tell me, "Don't go out looking for girls. Just wait it out and it will happen. If you go out looking for women it will lead to heartbreak." He also taught me to always respect women and never hurt them in any way. A real man would never do that.

If ever I have children of my own I want to make sure they have a relationship with God. That relationship saved my life.

Raising Children 101

Raising children is the most important job anyone could ever have. You are completely and totally responsible for another human beings life from before they are born until they can be responsible for themselves (sometimes that is not for quite awhile). To be blunt, don't bring another human into this world if you can't even take care of yourself. Until you can give sacrificially to others and put others needs before your own you shouldn't even be doing anything with a girl that could create another life. Grow up and become a man first. Brandon would probably be one of the first to tell you that it takes more to being a father than getting a girl pregnant.

Having children is the biggest blessing and the biggest heartache all in one. It's not an easy task by any means. Too often couples get wrapped up in the warm fuzzy thoughts of having a baby and they don't think past that. Babies don't stay babies for long. What I'm about to say next will probably make you think, "Holy cow why would anyone want to have children!" But it's all part of reality. Too many people have kids and then don't want to have them. They can't undo having a child once they have this little human being. They find out it's time consuming and harder than what they thought.

So here's the reality. Babies are cute, and soft, and adorable while they're sleeping and in a good mood. Then the crying begins and it might go on for hours. You don't know what to do. You've tried changing their diaper, feeding them, rocking them, walking the floor with them and nothing works! You're tired and the crying just won't stop. Babies cry. Sometimes they tend to cry at the most inconvenient moments, like in the middle of the night or when you go out to eat. A baby's cry is not something to ever be embarrassed about. Not only do babies cry, but they spit up on you. That really awesome shirt, that is your favorite, will be drooled on, vomited on, peed on, and possibly even pooped on. Babies are messy.

But, babies grow up to be toddlers. This is a fun stage! They start crawling, then walking, and you're so proud of them. Put your running shoes on now and don't take them off until they graduate (if even then, for you don't ever stop being a parent for the rest of your life). At this point, if you turn your back for a second, they are sure to get into something! They are curious, and life is an adventure for them! This stage takes lots of patience...wait...pretty much being a parent takes lots of patience. They will start to talk, and it will melt your heart the first time they say Dada.

Before you know it, they are two years old. Then they learn a new word that won't melt your heart so much. Because they hear it all the time, one of the first words they learn to say back to you is NO! You don't have to get mad at them for telling you no. Remember, you are the dad and you are bigger. If you tell them to "come here" and they say no, get up and go get them and tell them yes. Temper tantrums should not be tolerated. This happens a lot at this age. Be firm with you child in this matter and let them know it is not acceptable. Whenever my kids would try, to as we say in my family, "pitch a fit," it was dealt with immediately. Don't ignore it. Ignoring your child does not teach them right from wrong. If I was out in public and this happened I would pick my child up and tell them, "Because you are acting this way we are leaving. This is not how we act in a store/restaurant," and we would leave. If you say something like that, make sure you follow through. It might be a bit frustrating to you, but it's a teachable moment for them and an important one. If you're at home, tell them, "This is not how we behave and no one wants to watch or hear this, so until you're done you can be alone." Make sure they are in a safe setting where they can't get hurt, but leave them alone. If this doesn't work, then as a last resort spank them. A spanking should never be done in anger though. If you are angry, give yourself a little time out before taking action. Children are much smaller than you and in anger you may unintentionally hurt them. Before I spanked my kids I would tell them, "You are going to get a spanking. Do you know what you did wrong?" In doing this I was teaching them at a young age to take responsibility for their actions. You have to start as early as possible teaching your children right from wrong and to make right choices. This all sounds fun doesn't it? But it's all part of being a parent. You have to be an active participant in your child's life.

Your child turns three. They have a pretty good vocabulary by now and the attitude to go with it. It's an exciting time though! This age is a time where they really start learning things.

Read to them every day. Routines are important to kids. As a baby, from day one, try to keep a routine. This gives children a sense of security. When my babies were born, our routine at night was to give them a bath (every night), feed them, and rock them while reading or singing, then put them to bed. This would continue on with slight changes.

Develop a set bedtime and do not stray from it. My kids' bedtime, when they were young, was eight o'clock. At seven o'clock it was bath time; every night. I always tried to make their bed time a fun experience, so starting with bath time we would tell stories or listen to music. Don't let your kids get hyper during this time. It's a time to calm down and get ready for sleep. They would brush their teeth while I sang the alphabet song a couple of times through (this gave them a good idea of how long to brush their teeth). Then, one of my favorite times would come. After they are all cleaned up, and jammies were on, they would climb in bed and I would lie beside them; we would say our prayers and I would read them a story. One story, then music was turned on softly and I would kiss their foreheads, tell them, "Sleep with angels, I love you," turn out the light and leave. Sometimes they would get out of bed. I would allow this once and then I would lead them back to bed. Kids have fears and insecurities sometimes. Don't spank your child for getting out of bed. If you have set a good routine for them then they will go to bed. Yes, they might get up once or if their sharing a room you might hear giggles or whispers. First off, cherish the giggles. It means they're happy. But give them a warning to quiet down and go to sleep. Bedtimes have always been a special time for me. It's a time when my kids would open up and talk to me. Be a part of this with your children. You want them to feel close to you and able to talk to you.

So, now they are ready to start school. Seems like a natural process that should be easy. This is where parenting tends to get harder. Now the majority of their day is spent under the influence of others. This is why those first few years it is important to develop a good relationship with your child and instill in them right and wrong. Just because your child is in school do NOT slack on your parenting responsibilities. It is NOT the schools job to raise your child. Make sure you or your wife feeds them breakfast, every day. Make sure they have clean clothes. Make sure they have lunch, whether it is a packed lunch or a school lunch. Make sure, when they come home from school, you or your wife asks them about their day. Ask questions that they have to answer such as, "What was your favorite part of the day?" Don't ask a yes or no question. The point of this is to get your child to communicate with you or your wife. I loved picking my kids up from school. It was our alone time in the car where I had their undivided attention for a while and could talk to them. Know what's going on in their lives; who their friends are, who their coaches are, and who their teachers are. You are the parent. This is your responsibility. Stay in a routine during their school years. My kids would come home, have a snack, and before the TV came on or friends came over, homework needed to be done. Help them set priorities. These little routines that you are developing are actually very valuable teaching moments that will shape your child's life. I wanted my kids to know their education was their first priority. It's what will pay off in the long run in life.

Now Jr. High hits. You're going to start seeing some pretty big changes in your child. They become awkward.

Not quite a little kid anymore but not old enough to be an adult. Their bodies are changing and their hormones are making their presence known. They tend to pull away from you a little bit. Don't let them pull too far. In this day and age we are living in it is so important that we be a strong presence in our children's lives. Long before they enter Jr. High, you and your wife should have talked openly about sex to them. Don't let this be an embarrassing subject, but one that is discussed openly and honestly. When your kids come to you asking questions, be honest with them. Don't make this subject a laughing matter or a joking time. How you treat it will be the mindset they will have about it.

Don't leave it up to the schools to educate your children on their morals. The subjects of sex, drinking, drugs, and smoking should be taught by you and your spouse.

Tell them about the changes that will take place BEFORE they take place with their bodies. Don't use crude or vulgar language with your children when doing this. Be respectful. Tell them sex was intended for a husband and wife and explain to them how tempting it will be to NOT wait for marriage, but let them know the benefits of waiting. Don't just tell them not to do something without explaining why. Let them ask questions, and don't make them feel dumb or weird for asking. Your children should be able to come to you with anything. If they can't they will find someone else. That someone else may not have the same values as you.

Ok, we've made it to high school now! It's so tempting to want to be your child's best friend. These next few years can be kind of rough. Their friends now have a bigger influence over them then you do. Your child will have many friends, but only one dad. Be the dad. Be the parent. We want our kids to love us and to like us, but sometimes being the parent means loving your child enough to be hated. Know who your kids' friends are and who is influencing them. Make sure you have rules that they MUST obey. Don't just let your teenager do whatever they want. They still need your guidance. Yes, you do need to let them make choices. But just like when they were younger, you have to let them be responsible for their actions. They are still learning a lot in their high school years and the pressure is intense. By setting up rules, you are actually helping them to be the best they can be. They won't see this or understand. The high school years are known as the rebellious years. Even a child you have never had trouble with their entire life might all of a sudden make you want to pull your hair out! To help you out with the rule making I'm going to give you a few suggestions. The thing about rules though is if you're not consistent they won't follow them. One of the biggest life lessons you can teach your teenager is they don't always get what they want and they shouldn't expect things to just be given to them. They have to work hard for the things they want in life. If you want to win at a sport you work hard and focus. Same should go for anything else in life.

So, here are some "house rules for teenagers"

- Set a curfew for week days and weekends. They need to know they are not the only ones living in your house. You should not have to stay up worrying if your teen is OK because it's three in the morning and you don't know where they are. Or, you shouldn't be woken up by your teen coming in late when you have to get up and work the next morning. They have GOT to be considerate of others.

- Everyone in the house should be expected to do chores.

You can actually start this habit at a very young age. Your teen should not have to be told to do their chores. But, you will probably remind them anyway. Make sure they do them. Don't tell them to do them and then do them yourself. This isn't teaching them anything.

- Computers...Computers should be kept in a public room in the house. Not in the bedroom. There is a lot of nasty stuff out there you don't want your kids getting involved in or addicted to. Plus, there are people on line who are out to target teens and exploit them. Having the computer public just helps you to help them. Set time limits on how long they can be one it. Let them know that at any time you can check what they are doing. Again, this isn't to be controlling but to protect them. Get a good internet protection program that blocks all questionable sites.

- Kids are getting cell phones and iPad's at early ages. If you choose to give your child a cell phone or any other device in which they can chat with others on, make sure you let them know first off that you bought the phone and it technically belongs to you. If at any time you believe they are abusing it you will take away the privilege of having it. Giving your child a phone or computer at any age, and not teaching them the proper way to use it is irresponsible. There was a mother who gave her son an iPhone when he was thirteen. She made him sign a contract in order to have it. This is what the contract said:

"Merry Christmas! You are now the proud owner of an iPhone. You are a good & responsible 13-year-old boy and you deserve this gift. But with the acceptance of this present comes rules and regulations. Please read through the following contract.

I hope that you understand it is my job to raise you into a well-rounded, healthy young man that can function in the world and coexist with technology, not be ruled by it. Failure to comply with the following list will result in termination of your iPhone ownership. I love you madly & look forward to sharing several million text messages with you in the days to come.

1. It is my phone. I bought it. I pay for it. I am loaning it to you. Aren't I the greatest?"

2. I will always know the password.

3. If it rings, answer it, it is a phone. Say hello, use your manners. Do not ever ignore a phone call if the screen reads 'Mom' or 'Dad'. Not ever.

4. Hand the phone to one of your parents promptly at 7:30pm every school night & every weekend night at 9:00pm. It will be shut off for the night and turned on again at 7:30am. If you would not make a call to someone's land line, wherein their parents may answer first, then do not call or text. Listen to those instincts and respect other families like we would like to be respected.

5. It does not go to school with you. Have a conversation with the people you text in person. It's a life skill. *Half days, field trips and after school activities will require special consideration.

6. If it falls into the toilet, smashes on the ground,

or vanishes into thin air, you are responsible for the replacement costs or repairs. Mow a lawn, babysit, and stash some birthday money. It will happen, you should be prepared.

7. Do not use this technology to lie, fool, or deceive another human being. Do not involve yourself in conversations that are hurtful to others. Be a good friend first or stay out of the crossfire.

8. Do not text, email, or say anything through this device you would not say in person.

9. Do not text, email, or say anything to someone that you would not say out loud with their parents in the room. Censor yourself.

10. No porn. Search the web for information you would openly share with me. If you have a question about anything, ask a person; preferably me or your father.

11. Turn it off, silence it, and put it away in public; especially in a restaurant, at the movies, or while speaking with another human being. You are not a rude person; do not allow the iPhone to change that.

12. Do not send or receive pictures of your private parts or anyone else's private parts. Don't laugh. Someday you will be tempted to do this despite your high intelligence. It is risky and could ruin your teenage/college/adult life. It is always a bad idea. Cyberspace is vast and more powerful than you. And it is hard to make

anything of this magnitude disappear—including a bad reputation.

13. Don't take a zillion pictures and videos. There is no need to document everything. Live your experiences. They will be stored in your memory for eternity.

14. Leave your phone home sometimes and feel safe and secure in that decision. It is not alive or an extension of you. Learn to live without it. Be bigger and more powerful that FOMO—fear of missing out.

15. Download music that is new or classic or different than the millions of your peers that listen to the same exact stuff. Your generation has access to music like never before in history. Take advantage of that gift. Expand your horizons.

16. Play a game with words or puzzles or brain teasers every now and then.

17. Keep your eyes up. See the world happening around you. Stare out a window. Listen to the birds. Take a walk. Talk to a stranger. Wonder without googling.

18. You will mess up. I will take away your phone. We will sit down and talk about it. We will start over again. You & I, we are always learning. I am on your team. We are in this together.

It is my hope that you can agree to these terms. Most of the lessons listed here do not just apply to the iPhone, but to life. You are growing up in a fast and ever changing world. It is exciting and enticing. Keep it simple every chance you get. Trust your powerful mind and giant heart above any machine. I love you. I hope you enjoy your awesome new iPhone. Merry Christmas!

Xoxoxoxo

Mom

This mother has my respect. I'm sure her kid was not thrilled about all the rules that came with the phone but she was teaching him valuable lessons and being an active parent in his life. He knows he is loved.

You for sure need to have rules about dating. I'm not a big fan of dating in high school. I think it is a major distraction and can mess up futures. I believe at this age it causes a lot of unnecessary drama and pain. I would much rather see kids having fun with groups of friends, involved in activities, and focusing on their school work. This time in their life is so precious and rare. It is the only time they get to just be with friends and hang out without a bunch of responsibilities tugging at them. When they date, that changes all of that. Kids get so over involved in creating that exclusive serious relationship that they miss out on just being a kid. You can never get that time back. Encourage them to just enjoy it while they can. There is plenty of time for dating. But, if you decide to let your children date then you better have some clear guidelines and stick to them. You should know who they are dating and their boyfriend/girlfriend's family. If they are never bringing their date to your house then there might be a problem.

This is the time they start doing something that will scare the noodles out of you. Driving! Show them how to take care of their car. Let them know it's a privilege to have a car and to drive.

During their high school years your child will argue with you it seems like about everything. They will think you are the dumbest person they have ever met. They will roll eyes, slam doors, give you the silent treatment, and push your limits. Love them any ways. They are trying to become adults.

Now comes the hard part. Watching them pack up and leave for college. From the time they were born until now you should have constantly been an active participant in their lives. Real men are. You have been teaching them and training them to be the best person they can be. Give them their wings and let them fly. But make sure they know they always have a home in your heart. Here is one of those times where your heart will break. For years, every day they have been there. Now they won't be. You remember everything. You hear their voice, their laughter, their loud music and arguments with siblings. You remember their hugs and even the fights. When they come home on breaks you relish every little detail and moment with them. Then you discover a new phase they are in; the "know it all" phase. See, they now are college educated and know everything there is to know about life. Just tolerate this stage. It won't be long before they discover how little they really do know.

You feel like your job as a parent is almost over. But it's not. College is over and your child is now an adult with a career and family of their own. An amazing thing happens if you have stayed involved. They become one of your closest friends. They will seek your advice and will call you just because they miss "home."

Have you noticed that this is the longest subject I've written on? That's because raising children is more than just having them. It's a HUGE responsibility. You are responsible for the way another human being lives. Don't take the decision to have children lightly. You don't have children to make yourself feel good. You have children when you are ready to put yourself aside for the sake of others.

(Griff Schoen) "Only you can choose how your kids will turn out. Just because you had an unhappy home life as a child does not mean you will be a bad parent. My dad was an alcoholic, so he wasn't always available when I needed him. He never once went to one of my football games. I decided as a dad that I would make it to my kids sporting events as often as possible. Also, you are not your kid's best friend. You are their parent. Discipline is necessary if you want kids who are respectful and less likely to get into trouble later on. We have always been strict with discipline and folks constantly tell us what good kids we have. It's not a coincidence."

If you grew up in a bad home life then you know for certain how awful it was for you. Don't make the same mistakes. Your kids should know, without a doubt, you will be there for them. You should be their loudest fan at any event they are involved in. You should embarrass them with how many pictures you take of them. Your number one job is to provide for them. It's not anyone else's job. If you can't work and provide for your kids then don't have kids. Go to their school. Volunteer to do things with their class. Attend parent/teacher meetings. Know what their grades are. Don't make the excuse that you don't have time. Make time. This is why it is so important for you to know before you bring a new life into this world what your motives are. Can you give up your time for yourself in order to sit through a dance recital?

> (Stephanie Schraeder) "Treasure every moment, you never know when they will cease to happen. Remember that you were a child once, too, and let him out sometimes to play with your children. Teach your children how to show respect by respecting others. Date your little girl, sing to her, learn how to do her hair, and remember she is your princess and will be some other man's queen one day. Show your little boy how to date his mom. Play with him, wrestle and race, but let him win sometimes. Read to him, show him how to fix stuff, and let him 'hang out with you. And remember, he will love a Queen one day'"

Before you make the decision to have children, you need to realize that things don't go as we sometimes perfectly plan. Sometimes we don't have children with ten perfect finger and ten perfect toes. Pregnancy and childbirth is risky. A lot can go wrong. Are you willing to be able to live with that if it happens? You have to decide how strong of a person are you? Are you strong enough to be a parent? What if something happens?

My friend had a beautiful little girl they nicknamed Boo. They adored her so very much. She was an angel of a girl with a devilish streak in her that came from having two older brothers. One day, when "Boo" was seven, they were getting a shaved ice in a parking lot stand. "Boo" heard a train coming across the highway and jumped up from the picnic table her family was sitting at enjoying their treat to see it. The highway was a busy one with lots of cattle trucks rumbling past. The tiny little girl was quite a ways away from where her family sat. What she and her family didn't realize was that she had run behind an SUV. "Boo" was below the mirror level for the vehicle and the lady didn't see her when she started backing up. She was hit and run over. She somehow was still living. After being rushed to the hospital the doctor came into a room where I was waiting with my friend, "Boo's" mother, to hear what was being done. The doctor came in and sat down next to her and took her hand. He basically told her that she had been crushed from her toes to her head. Multiple broken and shattered bones and she was bleeding from her ears, nose, mouth and eyes. They needed to fly her to a bigger hospital, but could not do that until they got the bleeding under control and they were not able to do that, but were trying still.

They asked my friend and her husband to come back to the ER to see her. The rest of us (most of the church they attended were there for them) sat waiting for news. I will never forget what happened. This sweet little girl's parents entered the room. Her daddy was a large teddy bear of a man. He stood before us and in a quiet steady voice said, "Her hearts beating because it doesn't know to stop yet. It won't be long until she is with her Heavenly Father."

That day changed their lives. I watched them go through many struggles trying to make sense of it all. Only because of their Faith in God and the impact their sweet daughter had on others' lives were they able to continue day after day. I know it was not easy on them and I'm sure if you were to ask them today they would still tell you the hurt is there and pain of missing her still makes its presence known.

Here are wise words my friend advised, "Treasure every moment, you never know when they will cease to happen." This not only applies to your children, but to all those you hold close to your heart.

If you do have children, you will soon realize you will blink and they grow up. It truly does happen that fast. Play with them. Be silly! Dance with your daughter. Show her how a guy should respect her. Let her know she is beautiful just the way she is. Take her on dates; just the two of you. Let her know that you are the keeper of her heart, and until the two of you together find the right man for her you will be protecting that heart ferociously. She needs to know her daddy is her number one protector.

Play ball with your son. Yes, you will be tempted to tell glory stories of your high school days. That's OK, but keep in mind to not constantly be doing this. It could make him feel you think less of him if he's not as good as you were. Let him know it's not OK to talk about girls in a negative way. Teach him to respect them. Teach your son that he does not need a girl on his arm to be of value. Protect his heart also. Girls today are aggressive. Many good men have been destroyed because of the ploys of a female.

Show him how to work hard for what he wants.

Teach them to be strong in God. Take them to church. Let them attend church camps. Their faith and yours will need to be strong in this world. This should be your number one priority as a parent. If they don't know who God is personally then you have failed.

> (Coach Lance Roweton) "Raising your children is the most important thing you will do in your life. If you have boys, teach them how to be a man. If you have girls, be the man that gives them self-confidence and shows them how they are to be treated. Don't be afraid to discipline. Don't be afraid to spank. Teach them that it is OK to fail...as long as they tried their best. Remember that you do know best. Guide your kids in their

decision making when needed. Remember it is not what you do for your kids but rather what you do for themselves. Spend time with your kids and tell them you love them every chance you get."

Love, love, love them. Unconditionally! They did not asked to be brought into this world. That was your choice. When they make choices that don't please you, love them any ways. No parent should ever turn their backs on their child for no reason.

(Paul Dillman) "I raised six children and two step children of my own. Teaching them and disciplining them when they were young made it much easier in life. Train your children when they are young. Ignoring them and letting them do whatever they want makes it much harder in their middle years to obey you. All my children have grown up to show me respect and trust in guidance, and they all have made something out of themselves and depend upon themselves. Training a child young goes a long ways. Don't have kids until you know you can afford to give them a good home, time, love and time to be there for them when they need you."

(Gina Green) "Wait until you're 30 to have kids. I'm not kidding."

Let yourself grow up some before you decide to try to grow someone else up. It is WAY better to wait and have children when you are older. Your twenties should be a time when you are getting yourself together and preparing for your future family. Don't rush the steps. Raising kids is expensive. As of now the average cost to raise a child is about $300,000. This includes food, clothing, health care and various expenses. It does not include gifts, vacations, entertainment or college.

If you are going to have a child, then you need to make sure you can afford it. They are not a puppy. If you can't even afford a pet then you should not even be considering a child. Do not expect the government or anyone else to pay for your child. If you don't have money saved, if you don't have a permanent home, if you don't have a steady job, and if you don't have spare time, then don't have a child.

The more mature you are when you have a child the more wisdom you will have to raise your child with. Grow up first. Find out who you are first.

> (Papa & Granny) "When it comes time to raising children remember they are a blessing from God. You are to guide them in their schooling and in home life. Give lots of hugs and kisses and always tell them how proud you are of them and how much you love them. Do not be afraid to correct them when they do wrong, but in a loving way. Beating them is not the way."

My kids never doubted I loved them. I tell them ALL the time. I don't just tell them, but I show them with hugs and kisses and little things I know they enjoy. Even when I had to spank them, when they were younger, I always hugged them afterward and told them I did not like what they did, but I loved them.

They need to hear from their dad that they are loved. If not, they will find someone else to tell them.

> (Barry Farr) "Raising a child is about giving yourself away. We are surrounded in our culture with selfishness. Raising a child properly requires sacrifices but every sacrifice is worth it. They must

know that you are there for them no matter what and love them even if you do not see eye to eye."

Random Advice

If you have a son...

- Let him drive. Every child remembers the first time they drove on daddy's lap. For that one moment, he will believe that he is just like you.

- Teach him to be picky; especially when it comes to women and steak. Teach him to never settle for second best.

- Take him to a ball game. There is something about sharing a day of hot dogs, sunshine and baseball with your father.

- Love with Bravery. Boys have this preconceived notion that they have to be tough. When he is young, he will express his love fully and innocently. As he grows, he will hide his feelings and wipe off kisses. It takes courage for a man to show love; teach him to be courageous.

- Talk together. Talk about anything. Let him tell you about friends and school. Listen. Ask questions. Share dreams, hopes, and concerns.

- Teach him manners. Teach him how to be a gentleman. It's a dying art.

- Teach him when to stand up and when to walk away. He should know that he doesn't have to throw punches to prove he is right. He may not always be right. Make sure he knows how to demand respect- he is worthy of it. It does not mean he has to fight back with fists or words, because sometimes you say more with silence.

- Teach him to choose his battles. Make sure he knows which battles are worth fighting—like for family or God. Remind him people can be mean and nasty because of jealousy, or other personal reasons. Help him to understand when to shut his mouth and walk-away. Teach him to be the bigger person.

- Teach him there are moments to be completely ridiculous. Do something silly with him.

- Let him win. Sometimes he needs to know that big things are possible.

- Teach him about family. Let him know family is always worth fighting for. Family is always worth standing up for. At the end of the day, he has you to fall back on.

- Father him. Remind him over and over that no one will ever love him like you love him.

- Listen to him now. If you don't listen to the little things now, he won't share the big things later.

- Give him bear hugs. The kind that squeezes his insides and makes him giggle. The kind of hug only a daddy can give.

- Grow a big belly. Because every child should get the chance to rest their rear on the absolute softest pillow ever. Daddy's belly is the best place to land.

- Don't say it, do it. American inventor Charles F. Kettering once said, "Every father should remember that one day his son will follow his example instead of his advice." Be a good one.

- Be his hero. You are anyway. Don't disappoint. Prove to him that a dad is the biggest hero of all. Only dads can save the day.

- Teach him to keep his eyes on the ball and follow through, both in sports and in life.

- Speaking of sports, teach him to pick a team and stick with them. There are few things more important in life than loyalty. It's a dying trait currently in short supply.

- Good fathers make good sons.

If you have a daughter...

The following are some life lessons you might like to pass on to your own daughter some day:

- When posing for any photos, assume that the only people who will see them are your parents, your boss, and the dean of admissions.

- Life is too short not to order fries.

- Never date a man who is rude to waiters, doesn't say, "bless you" when you sneeze, or won't offer you his jacket when you're cold.

- Don't worry about being popular. The "weird" kids are much more fun and will end up being your most interesting friends. Also, when it comes to friends, you can't trump quality with quantity. Choose wisely. A person is what his company is. Friend's influence one's thinking, so choose your friends with care and stay away from bad company.

- Give charitably, generously, and anonymously.

- Never cheat. Not on exams, the crossword puzzle, or your boyfriend.

- If you love someone, tell them. Don't hold back.

- It may be a small world but it's a huge planet. Grab every opportunity to see as much of it as you possibly can. Most people don't.

- Never regret staying home alone with a good book.

- If you feel the need to reinvent yourself, at least be original. No pink hair unless you join the circus.

- Learn from the bad as well as the good. Fall down, make a mess, break something occasionally. And always remember the story is never over.

- Don't make a scene.

- Learn how to entertain yourself. Close the door, crank up the stereo, and dork out. Invent new dance moves. Play the air guitar. many people are self-conscious even when they're alone. Don't be one of those people.

- While you're at it, learn to laugh at yourself.

- Don't waste your money on beauty magazines. They will only make you doubt your natural beauty.

- Remember that nice guys do finish first. If you don't know that, then you don't know where the finish line is.

- Learn to cook one thing really well.

- Happiness is not fame, money or power.

- Try to make friendships that will last a lifetime, male and female. Women and men can have friends of the opposite sex, they just have to define their friendship and their boundaries and keep them. There is no quicker way to ruin a friendship than sex.

- Life has many detours and pitfalls, small regrets for having given up some of our small dreams, but your big dreams should never be compromised.

Make traditions for your children. Holidays are a great time for this, but they don't have to be the only time. Have at least one meal a day at the kitchen table as a family. Spend this time talking about your day, listening to their day, asking questions, and laughing together. Meal time as a family is a dying tradition, and it's one that I believe families cannot afford to let die. We live in a fast paced busy world that steals our families away from us. Fight for your time with them. Insist on special quality times.

Christmas is one of my favorite Holiday traditions with my children. When they were little, it started with putting up the Christmas tree the day after Thanksgiving. On Christmas Eve we would bake a Birthday cake for Jesus then, that night, as they went to bed, every year I would read them, "T'was The Night Before Christmas." They wrote letters to Santa and left them out with milk and cookies. After they were asleep, I would answer the letters, my husband would eat some of the cookies (we always left bites from Santa), and we put gifts under the tree. Christmas day after gifts were opened and meals were eaten, later that night we would read the real Christmas story out of the Bible and eat birthday cake. I always wanted my kids to know what the real meaning of Christmas was.

Whatever your traditions are, find something that is special to you and be faithful in doing it every year with your children. It's what memories are made of. Use your imagination and don't be afraid to be silly. They will cherish these moments over everything else.

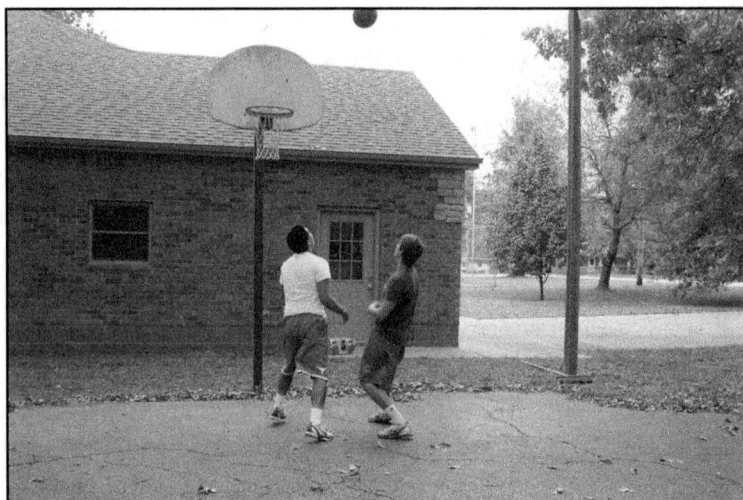

Tim and Tyler shooting hoops

Chapter 17

FROM A MOTHER'S HEART

Twenty Things a Mom Should Tell Her Son:

1. Play a sport.

2. It will teach you how to win honorable, lose gracefully, respect authority, work with others, manage your time and stay out of trouble.

3. You will set the tone for the sexual relationship, so don't take something away from her you can't give back.

5. Save money when you're young because you're going to need it someday.

6. Know how to use the dishwasher, oven, washing machine, iron, vacuum, mop and broom.

7. Pray and be a spiritual leader.

8. Don't ever bully someone or start a fight. But if someone starts one by hitting you then make sure you finish it. In other words, defend yourself.

9. Your knowledge and education is something no one can ever take away from you.

10. Treat women kindly.

11. Take pride in your appearance.

12. Be strong and tender at the same time.

13. A woman can do everything you can do. This includes her having a successful career and you changing diapers at 3 A.M. Mutual respect is the key to a good relationship.

14. "yes ma'am: and "yes sir" still go a long way.

15. The reason that they're called "private parts" is because they're "private." Please do not scratch them in public.

16. Peer pressure is a scary thing. Be a good leader and others will follow.

17. Bringing her flowers for no reason is always a good idea.

18. It is better to be kind than to be right.

19. A sense of humor goes a long way in the healing process.

20. Please choose your spouse wisely. She is the gatekeeper for your "mom" to get to spend time with you and your children.

Remember to call your "mom" because she just might be missing you.

Conclusion

The End is Just the Beginning

"Then we will no longer be immature like children. We won't be tossed and blown about by every wind of new teaching. We will not be influenced when people try to trick us with lies so clever they sound like the truth. Instead, we will speak the truth in love, growing in every way more and more like Christ, who is the head of his body, the church" (Ephesians 4:14-15).

The Road Not Taken

Two roads diverged in a yellow wood,

And sorry I could not travel both

And be one traveler, long I stood

And looked down one as far as I could

To where it bent in the undergrowth;

Then took the other, as just as fair,

And having perhaps the better claim,

Because it was grassy and wanted wear;

Though as for that, the passing there

Had worn them really about the same,

And both that morning equally lay

In leaves no step had trodden black.

Oh, I kept the first for another day!

Yet knowing how way leads on to way,

I doubted if I should ever come back.

I shall be telling this with a sigh

Somewhere ages and ages hence;

Two roads diverged in a wood, and I-

I took the one less traveled by,

And that has made all the difference.

The above poem is about choices in life. You will have to make many choices throughout your life both big and little. Even choosing not to do anything is still a choice (usually a lazy one but still a choice). Those choices not only affect you but those around you. They also may not affect you in small ways but in ways that will change your life.

Make your choices carefully. As the poem says, once you have chosen a path it may be very difficult to go back to the other path if the one you chose was wrong.

No one can go back and make a brand new start. Anyone can start from now and make a brand new ending.

> (Coach Lance Roweton) "...Remember, your journey is just beginning. Your life is getting ready to change forever and you will forever become a man in the process. Please take any advice given in this piece that you feel applicable to your life and run with it."

You're almost finished with this book. I, along with many others, have called out the man in you. I have faith that you will be a wonderful, Godly man. Never tune out advice given to you. Listen and apply it where you need to. Above everything seek God's will for your life. Listen to Him.

I once had a young man who would get so upset whenever someone would say God spoke to them. He would shake his hands in the air and say, "So God literally stood in front of them and talked to them!"

I'm sure God didn't literally stand in front of them and speak. Although He sure could if He so chose to. So how does God speak to us? There are countless ways! God can speak to us through His written Word, through the wisdom of others, through crazy ladies who sometimes talks to kids no one else wants to be around, and through the miracles all around us.

I know many who have been dealt a hard life who don't believe in miracles. Go outside and stand. Close your eyes and listen to life. Listen really carefully. You can hear the miracles all around you. Psalm 46:10 says, "Be still and know that I am God." Now go on right now. Yes, put the book down and go outside and be still and listen. Did you hear that? It's God's whisper in the wind. Did you hear birds singing? It's His song He gives to you every day. Maybe you hear children playing and laughing somewhere or dog's barking. It's His creation, the gift of life. Open your eyes and look around. Do you see all the beauty, all the different textures and colors? Look up at the sky and notice what all you can really see, then look down at the ground to the tiniest detail. What amazing colors are on His palate! God is speaking to you. He is telling you He created all of this because of His great love for you.

Have you ever had someone say something to you or do something for you and they just can't explain why? Sometimes people will do things for you and you're not even aware of it being done. That's God using others.

I know the past can hurt and life can seem pretty bad. We tend to focus on all the negative things in life and forget the goodness of God. Just know that God is speaking to you daily, and He is telling you He cares. Next time you are feeling the injustice of the world on your back, try letting God use you to help someone else. When you do this you will see how easy it is to forget your own problems and be filled with joy over doing something life-changing for someone else.

(Coach Daniel Bayless) "Let me pass on some of the best advice I ever got. It was from one of the most successful men I have ever met. He said there are two roads in life; one starts easy and gets harder, the other starts harder and gets easy. He is right...If you do things the right way and don't take short cuts it pays off in the long run and your road will get easier."

An elderly carpenter was ready to retire. He told his employer/contractor of his plans to leave the house building business and live a more leisurely life with his wife enjoying his extended family. He would miss the paycheck, but he needed to retire. They could get by.

The contractor was sorry to see his good worker go and asked if he could build just one more house as a personal favor. The carpenter said yes, but in time it was easy to see that his heart was not in his work. He resorted to shoddy workmanship and used inferior materials. It was an unfortunate way to end his career.

When the carpenter finished his work and the builder came to inspect the house, the contractor handed the front-door key to the carpenter. "This is your house," he said, "my gift to you."

What a shock! What a shame! If he had only known he was building his own house, he would have done it all so differently. Now he had to live in the home he had built none too well.

This is how it is with us. We build our lives in a distracted way, reacting rather than acting, willing to put up less than the best. At important points we do not give the job our best effort. Then, with a shock, we look at the situation we have created and find that we are now living in the house we have built. If we had realized, we would have done it differently.

Think of yourself as the carpenter. Think about your house. Each day you hammer a nail, place a board, or erect a wall. Build it wisely. It is the only life you will ever build. Even if you live it for only one day more, that day deserves to be lived graciously and with dignity. Life is a do-it-yourself project; do it well.

(Coach Robby Hoegh) "The following is something I saw from John Maxwell on character that has been an impact in my own life and my perspective. I hope it will do the same for you.

- The circumstances amid which you live determine your reputation...the truth you believe, determines your character.

- Reputation is what you are supposed to be; character is what you are.

- Reputation is the photograph; character is the face.

- Reputation comes over one from without; character grows up from within.

- Reputation is what you have when you come to a new community; character is what you have when you go away.

- Your reputation is made in a moment; you character is built in a lifetime.

- Your reputation is learned in an hour; your character does not come to light for a year.

- Reputation grows like a mushroom; character lasts like eternity.

- Reputation is what men say about you on your tombstone; character is what the angels say about you before the throne of God."

The Star Fish Story

Adapted from *The Star Thrower* by Loren Eiseley (1907-1977)

Once upon a time, there was a wise man that used to go to the ocean to do his writing. He had a habit of walking on the beach before he began his work.

One day, as he was walking along the shore, he looked down the beach and saw a human figure moving like a dancer. He smiled to himself at the thought of someone who would dance to the day, and so, he walked faster to catch up.

As he got closer, he noticed that the figure was that of a young man, and that what he was doing was not dancing at all. The young man was reaching down to the shore, picking up small objects, and throwing them into the ocean.

He came closer still and called out 'Good morning! May I ask what it is that you are doing:'

The young man paused, looked up, and replied, 'Throwing starfish into the ocean.'

'I must ask, the, why are you throwing starfish into the ocean?' asked the somewhat startled wise man.

To this, the young man replied, 'The sun is up and the tide is going out. If I don't throw them in, they'll die.'

Upon hearing this, the wise man commented, 'But, young man, do you not realize that there are miles and miles of beach and there are starfish all along every mile? You can't possibly make a difference!'

At this, the young man bent down, picked up yet another starfish, and threw it into the ocean. As it met the water, he said, 'It made a difference for that one.'

To my children of my heart...I hope God has allowed me to make a positive difference in your life either big or small. Pay it forward.

I love you...
SWA...
Goodnight.

Tina/T/Momma T/Monkey

Endnotes

Chapter 14

1. *As for Me and My House* [Nashville; Thomas Nelson, 1990] p. 31

2. *Is This the One?* 9 Tests for Ma [InterVarsity Press] pp 6, Keith R. Anderson, 1996

3. *Fit to Be Tied* [Grand Rapids, Mich.: Zondervan, 1991] pp. 37-38

www.ingramcontent.com/pod-product-compliance
Lightning Source LLC
LaVergne TN
LVHW051053080426
835508LV00019B/1843